WALKING IN TICINO

LUGANO, LOCARNO AND THE MOUNTAINS OF SOUTHERN SWITZERLAND

by Andrew Beattie

JUNIPER HOUSE, MURLEY MOSS,
OXENHOLME ROAD, KENDAL, CUMBRIA LA9 7RL
www.cicerone.co.uk

Printed by Severn, Gloucester, on responsibly sourced paper.
A catalogue record for this book is available from the British Library.
All photographs are by the author unless otherwise stated.

Route mapping by Lovell Johns www.lovelljohns.com
Contains OpenStreetMap.org data © OpenStreetMap
contributors, CC-BY-SA. NASA relief data courtesy of ESRI

Updates to this guide

While every effort is made by our authors to ensure the accuracy of guide-books as they go to print, changes can occur during the lifetime of an edition. This guidebook was researched and written during the Covid-19 pandemic. While we are not aware of any significant changes to routes or facilities at the time of printing, it is likely that the current situation will give rise to more changes than would usually be expected. Any updates that we know of for this guide will be on the Cicerone website (www.cicerone.co.uk/1060/updates), so please check before planning your trip. We also advise that you check information about such things as transport, accom-modation and shops locally. Even rights of way can be altered over time.

We are always grateful for information about any discrepancies between a guidebook and the facts on the ground, sent by email to updates@cicerone.co.uk or by post to Cicerone, Juniper House, Murley Moss, Oxenholme Road, Kendal, LA9 7RL.

Register your book: To sign up to receive free updates, special offers and GPX files where available, register your book at www.cicerone.co.uk.

Front cover: This bridge in Bignasco is crossed towards the end of Walk 15

CONTENTS

Mountain safety

Every mountain walk has its dangers, and those described in this guidebook are no exception. All who walk or climb in the mountains should recognise this and take responsibility for themselves and their companions along the way. The author and publisher have made every effort to ensure that the information contained in this guide was correct when it went to press, but, except for any liability that cannot be excluded by law, they cannot accept responsibility for any loss, injury or inconvenience sustained by any person using this book.

International distress signal *(emergency only)*
Six blasts on a whistle (and flashes with a torch after dark) spaced evenly for one minute, followed by a minute's pause. Repeat until an answer is received. The response is three signals per minute followed by a minute's pause.

Helicopter rescue
The following signals are used to communicate with a helicopter:

Help needed:
raise both arms
above head to
form a 'Y'

Help not needed:
raise one arm
above head, extend
other arm downward

Emergency telephone numbers
If telephoning from the UK the dialling codes are:
Italy: 0039; *Switzerland:* 0041

Medical emergency number in Ticino (Ticino Soccorso): 144
Rega (Swiss Air-Rescue) has a base in Locarno; emergency number: 1414
Police emergency number: 117
General emergency number: 112
Road emergency and breakdown number: 140

Weather reports
Switzerland: see http://www.meteoswiss.admin.ch
or https://www.meteocentrale.ch

Mountain rescue can be very expensive – be adequately insured.

Picturesque Lavertezzo is at the start of walks 19 and 20, and the end of Walk 18

INTRODUCTION

The lakeside resort of Ascona is one of Ticino's major draws for tourists

In 1875 the great Alpine writer Douglas W. Freshfield wrote in his book *The Italian Alps* that 'Lago Maggiore is a name well known to thousands, but I doubt whether, even in the Alpine Club, ten could be found ready to point out off-hand the whereabouts of Valle Maggia (to its north). Yet the valley offers a type of beauty as rare and worth knowing as the lake into which its waters flow.' Nearly a century and a half later, much the same could be said: everyone seems to know Lake Maggiore – and Lake Lugano, close by – but few know of the fabulous Alpine scenery that surrounds these lakes.

The Valle Maggia is part of the Italian-speaking Swiss canton of Ticino, and just as in Freshfield's day, this part of the Alps is not well known to English-speaking visitors, and those who do know it tend to think of it as a 'lakes' destination rather than 'mountains'. The tourists in Ticino are overwhelmingly German speakers from Zurich, Basel or Frankfurt, who cross the spine of the Alps via the Gotthard tunnels from the cool climes of Northern Europe to experience the sweet scents, vibrant colours and blazing sunshine of the South. Ticino is Switzerland, to be sure, but with its Italian food and language, its warm summer weather and its stylish cities, it's Switzerland with a decisive Mediterranean twist. Lakes Lugano and Maggiore – and the palm-fringed resorts of Lugano and Locarno – are the draw for many, but beyond these cities – as Douglas Freshfield noted – there is fabulous mountain scenery, which attracts hundreds of thousands of walkers every year.

This book divides Ticino into four regions, each using a specific town or city as a base. The first section looks at walks around Lugano, right in the south of the Canton, where paths tend to take walkers along the lake shore or along ridges high above it. The second section describes walks accessible from Locarno, on Lake Maggiore, where the emphasis is less on lake views and more on high mountain scenery, for it is from Locarno that access can be most easily gained to the dramatic Cristallina range in the northwest of the Canton. The third section focuses on the towns of Bellinzona and Biasca, which lie on the main road and railway lines through the Canton, and provide access to relatively easy forest walks in the broad valley of the Ticino river as well as to more challenging walks through the wilder scenery of a beautiful side valley, the Val Blenio. The last section of the book describes walks through the dramatic scenery of the northern part of the Canton, around

Airolo and the St Gotthard Pass, where trails lie in the shadow of Ticino's highest and most snow-bound peaks.

Throughout the book the walks highlight the best that the Ticino countryside has to offer: ancient trails through stone villages characterised by colourful window boxes and cobbled lanes, lush narrow valleys that lie in the shadow of granite peaks, and forests of chestnut and silver birch that hide gushing waterfalls and crystal streams. The trails walkers follow are often former mule tracks used by traders, which, as they ascend beyond the high pastures and into raw mountain scenery, give way to rocky paths once trodden by hunters – all of which allow access to untamed nature rather than the crowded familiarity found in many other parts of Switzerland.

HISTORY

During the Iron and Bronze Ages the area that is today Ticino was settled by the Lepontii, a Celtic tribe whose main centres were at Oscela, now Domodossola in Italy, and Bilitio, now Bellinzona, the cantonal capital of Ticino. Their territory included the southern slopes of the St. Gotthard Pass and Simplon Pass. Later, probably during the rule of Augustus (27BC–14AD), the area became part of the Roman Empire. After the fall of the Western Empire, Ticino was ruled by Germanic tribes from northern Continental Europe – the Ostrogoths, the Lombards and the Franks, and in the early twelfth century Ticino became the focus of a territorial struggle which led to its eventual acquisition by the Dukes of Milan.

Switzerland itself was founded in 1291 when three rural communities situated around Lake Lucerne – Uri, Schwyz and Unterwalden – formed an alliance that later grew to include the cities of Lucerne, Zurich and Bern. During the fifteenth century the Swiss Confederates sought to expand their territory and gain independence from the Habsburg Empire. Between 1403 and 1422 some parts of Ticino were conquered and subsequently lost by forces from Canton Uri. A subsequent campaign was more successful: Uri conquered the Leventina Valley in

At the end of Walk 18 and the start of Walk 20, the routes cross this medieval arched bridge at Lavertezzo

the north of the Canton in 1440, and sixty years later forces from Cantons Schwyz and Nidwalden pushed on south and brought the town of Bellinzona under Confederate control. The Confederates had always controlled the northern approach to the St Gotthard Pass, one of the most important trade links over the Alps: now they controlled the southern approaches as well.

These Confederate victories in Ticino were finally consolidated in 1512 when Locarno, the Maggia Valley, Lugano and Mendrisio were annexed – creating the familiar wedge of Swiss territory (shaped like an inverted triangle) that to this day forms an arrow-head piercing northern Italy. These territories were the last to be conquered by the Swiss Confederation, which gave up further expansion after its defeat at the battle of Marignano in 1515 by Francis I of France.

For nearly three centuries the northern part of the region was ruled by Canton Uri while the southern part – including the main centres of Lugano and Locarno – was ruled directly by the Swiss Confederacy. Between 1798 and 1803, during the Helvetic Republic, Napoleon carved the region into two cantons (Bellinzona and Lugano) but in 1803, after Napoleonic rule ended, the two were unified to form the canton of Ticino, which joined the Swiss Confederation as a full member in the same year. Until 1878 the three largest cities,

Tourist boats on Lake Lugano give access to many walks in the first part of this book

Bellinzona, Lugano and Locarno, alternated as capital of the canton, but in 1878 Bellinzona became the permanent cantonal capital.

TICINO TODAY

By some measurement methods Switzerland has the highest living standards in the world – and Ticino is among the wealthiest cantons. The economy is based around services, particularly banking (Lugano is Switzerland's third-largest financial sector after Zurich and Geneva), while other noteworthy industries are gold refining and viticulture (many walks around Bellinzona run through vineyards growing grapes for Merlot wines). A large proportion of the

workforce are *frontalieri*, living in the Italian cities of Como and Varese and commuting across the border into Ticino each day.

Tourism is a major sector of the economy. Around 21 million tourists visit Ticino each year – a figure that includes day-visitors from Italy and German-speaking parts of Switzerland – and anyone visiting the Canton in summer will testify to Ticino's popularity with visitors. The lakeside cities of Lugano and Locarno, along with the latter's neighbouring resort of Ascona, provide the main draws. In winter the picture is rather different, with some low-key skiing at Bosco Gurin, Airolo and in the Val Blenio, but nowhere that could classify as a Verbier or St Moritz-style 'ski resort'

– the mountains are too low, and the weather this side of the Alps too warm, for there to be enough scope for 'serious' skiing.

A sizeable proportion of Ticino's residents – over a quarter – are foreign nationals. Of these, most are Italian, though there are also substantial minorities of Portuguese and Croats; the region's Italian heritage means that Roman Catholicism is the predominant religion.

GEOLOGY AND LANDSCAPE

Evidence of the great tectonic upheaval that formed the Alps is clearly visible in Ticino – specifically in a hamlet named Pianezzo, which is situated in the Morobbia valley just south of Bellinzona. Here a medieval bridge spans the rushing Morobbia torrent – and as it does so, it passes over horizontal beds of schist rock. Yet on the valley sides above the bridge is another rock type entirely – mica – whose deposits are laid down vertically. The mica was twisted into this position by tectonic forces that accompanied the collision of the African and Eurasian tectonic plates, which began some 80 million years ago; geologists point to the schists at Pianezzo being part of the African plate and the adjacent mica outcrops being part of the Eurasian plate – and so the ancient bridge, where contrasting rocks from the two colliding plates are actually exposed, is something of a pilgrimage place for them.

The geological acrobatics exposed at Pianezzo form a small section of what geologists know as the Insubric line. This is a 1000 km fault cutting east-west across the Southern Alps, marking the place where continental collision is still ongoing: in fact, this process lifts the mountains a little higher each year, while the line itself divides the limestone Alps to the south from the largely crystalline, metamorphic rocks to the north. Some of the material that has been churned upwards by the collision of the two plates is actually buckled-up sea floor, and at the summit of the San Bernardino Pass, which gives access to Ticino from northeastern Switzerland, are outcrops of a grey, slatey rock known as gneiss, which was once buried 100km down inside the earth.

During the Quaternary era – the most recent geological period, extending from 2.6m years ago to the present – the Alps have witnessed repeated cold periods during which ice has advanced, only to retreat during the warmer periods (such as the one we are living in now). The spectacular scenery of Ticino, and the rest of the Alps, owes much to the erosive power of this moving ice, which has created the distinctive steep-sided, flat-bottomed valleys such as the lower Ticino valley (best appreciated from the many walks that rise above Bellinzona, covered in part three of this book). The lakes that dominate the southern part of the region, Lugano and Maggiore, also have glacial origins: long, thin, spindly and very deep, they are the result of river water filling in glacially deepened valleys after the ice has retreated.

In terms of scenery, the further north you go the higher the mountains and the more rugged and wild the environment for walkers. The lowest point in Ticino is the shoreline of Lake Maggiore, which at 193m is the also lowest point in Switzerland, while at Chiasso, in the very south of the canton, the Alps come to an end and the flat plains of Northern Italy open up.

By contrast, the highest peak is Adula (3402m), more commonly known by its German name Rheinwaldhorn, which lies in northeastern Ticino on its border with the neighbouring Canton, Graubünden, and which forms part of a 'wall' of high peaks that separate Ticino from the rest of Switzerland (and which is best seen from walk 28). However, to reach its summit – and the summits of similarly lofty peaks – requires specialist climbing experience and equipment; the highest altitude reached by walks in this book is a rather more modest 2575m, which is the height of the mountain hut Capanna Cristallina, reached (from different directions) on walks 16 and 33.

PLANTS AND FLOWERS

The breadth of altitudes and habitats in Ticino give rise to a huge variety of plants, which include species associated with both high Alpine and with lower Mediterranean environments.

Ticino's deep, narrow lakes, including Lake Lugano (pictured from Walk 5), were formed by glacial erosion during the last period of ice advance

In fact, all over the Southern Alps, mountain species have colonised lowland areas, their seeds carried by the wind or streams, while some hardy Mediterranean species have found a home in mountain glens protected from winter frosts by warm southerly winds.

High meadows are often covered in colourful bloom while higher up white, yellow or pink flower heads can flourish amidst scree slopes and expansive cushion plants can drape themselves across rock surfaces. The most common species that walkers will see are gentians, instantly recognizable for their large, trumpet-like and intensely blue flowers emanating from a slender stem; and orchids, whose smaller but more numerous petals have a purple-pink hue and stand more prominently above the ground. *Alpenrose*, a dwarf rhododendron, is also common; these plants have characteristic deep pink to purple flowers and dark green elliptical leaves, but do not stand upright in the way that orchids do. If you are walking above 1800m you may be lucky enough to see an edelweiss (*stella alpina* in Italian), the daisy-like flower that is the national emblem of Switzerland: experts will tell you that it is not really a flower as such, but a set of 500 to a thousand tiny florets grouped in several heads (between 2 and 10 of them) surrounded by 5 to 15 white velvety leaves.

Mention too must be made of the planted subtropical gardens that

Gentians are typical flowers seen on walks (photo: David Short, Wikimedia Commons)

occupy many lakeside locations in Ticino (and neighbouring parts of Italy): lush with basins of waterlillies and stands of tall palm trees, giant figs or beautiful succulents (such as cacti), these gardens are must-visit for any plant-lover – and Walk 3 passes right through one of them (the Parco San Grato), ending close to another, the Parco Scherrer in Morcote.

The best time to experience Ticino's floral beauty is from spring to mid-July, though flowers can still brighten walks from late-July right through October – when the woods that cover many of the Canton's lower valleys are bathed in autumnal golds and auburns. Remember, though, that flowers are protected by law and that picking them is often forbidden. Walk carefully around stands of flowers, but after taking time to photograph them, study them or breathe their heady perfumes, leave them for others to enjoy. If you want to know more, Cicerone's pocket-sized guide *Alpine Flowers* by Gillian Price is excellent for identifying plants when 'in the field', and is crammed full of detail and photographs.

WILDLIFE

The most common animal seen by walkers in Ticino is the marmot, a cute, fat, furry rodent that lives in hillside colonies and which was known to Romans as the 'alpine mouse' (in fact it's a member of the squirrel family). Marmots grow to be the size of a large hare and live among boulder slopes and upper pastures – anywhere that offers cover for their burrows. They hibernate in winter and emerge in springtime when they mate; their young are born during the early summer and can be seen romping or play-fighting in short grass. Their most distinctive feature is the loud, shrill whistle that is emitted by a marmot acting as a 'sentry' for the colony, who stands upright and alert like a meerkat as the others forage for food. Whistles warn of approaching walkers – and on occasions of hovering birds of prey too. When it sounds the marmots will dive for cover into their burrows, leaving the approaching walker with a view of a succession of furry behinds disappearing into the ground.

An Alpine Marmot (photographed in the French Alps): these intriguing creatures are often seen by walkers around the tree line (photo: DavAnubis, Wikimedia Commons)

Chamois are rather more elusive and are rarely seen at close quarters. They are goat-like creatures with tawny coats and curving horns and they inhabit high pastureland around the snowline. Sometimes a herd can be seen from a distance picking its way with agility through steep terrain.

Other creatures include red squirrels, foxes, hares, deer, and wild boar. The latter are hairy brown pigs with prominent ears, and make their homes amidst deciduous and mixed woodland – you might see hoof prints in the mud on forest tracks, but the only sight or sound of a boar you are likely to have is of a dark form crashing away through the undergrowth, emitting a series of grunts as it does so. They are hardy, adaptable and intelligent, but are considered a nuisance as they trample and eat crops and are hunted during the months of September to January. In a very small minority of cases, they have been known to be a danger to humans.

In the sky you might be lucky enough to hear – or even see – eagle owls and capercaillie, whose call can be heard ringing through woodlands at dawn in springtime. Above the treeline golden eagles make their homes on rock ledges, from which they make raids on marmot colonies – their chief source of food in summer.

That said, the most 'wildlife' walkers will encounter is, not surprisingly, farm animals, in the form of cattle and, on higher pastures, sheep and goats; many paths run straight through fields and enclosures for animals, which are protected by electric fences, though there's always a gate that walkers can open and close to pass through them (with an insulator so you don't get an electric shock).

GETTING THERE

Ticino lies at the heart of Europe, on one of the continent's major international road and rail arteries (linking Milan and Zurich) – making it easily accessible by land routes from Germany and Italy. Europe's dense motorway and rail network means that access from France and other countries in Northern Europe is also straightforward. The following section focuses on surface routes to Ticino from the UK and Ireland and air routes from there and the rest of the world.

By train
It's possible to travel from London to Ticino in a day (though travelling from other parts of the UK would require an overnight stop). The journey can be done in three stages – London to Paris (Gare du Nord) on Eurostar (2 hr 15 min on the fastest trains), Paris (Gare de Lyon) to Zurich by TGV (4 hours), and then Zurich to Airolo, Bellinzona, Locarno or Lugano (2–3 hours). Timetables can be viewed and tickets bought on www.thetrainline.com.

By car
You can bring your car to Switzerland from Ireland or the UK by one of

Caslano, viewed from the path along the Lake Lugano shoreline (Walk 4)

the many ferry services (www.dfds. com; www.stenaline.co.uk; www. irishferries.com; www.brittany-ferries.co.uk). Alternatively you can travel with your car on the train from the UK through the Channel Tunnel (www.eurotunnel.com). The drive from Calais down to Ticino (the fastest route is via Reims, Metz, Strasbourg, Basel and Lucerne) should take between nine and ten hours. You will approach Ticino from the North, via the Gotthard Pass (open June to November) or the Gotthard road tunnel (open all year). Other passes include the Lucomagno (Lukmanier), which links Ticino with northeast Switzerland, and the Novena (Nufenen), the highest pass wholly within Switzerland, which links Ticino and Canton Valais, to the northwest.

The motorway system in Switzerland is first class, but you need to purchase a vignette (valid on all motorways for a year) to use them: buy one online at www.swiss-vignette.co.uk or at the border (you need an additional vignette for trailers and caravans). Note that drivers must carry a red warning triangle, their national driving licence (or an international drivers' licence) and the vehicle's insurance documents, and that third party insurance is compulsory.

Malpensa airport

Milan Malpensa Airport, situated 49km Northwest of Milan, is by far the most convenient major international airport for Ticino. It's the busiest in Northern Italy, with flights to destinations in Asia, Africa and North America as well as within Europe. British Airways, Aer Lingus, Ryanair and Easyjet fly there from a number of cities in the UK and Ireland (in fact Easyjet has up to 6 daily flights into this airport from London Gatwick). There are direct, hourly trains to Bellinzona (1 hr 55 min) and Lugano (1 hr 40 min) from both terminals, and buses too to Lugano and other towns in Ticino, which take less time than the train and are cheaper – see www.luganoservices.ch for the latter.

Bergamo and Linate airports

Bergamo airport (also known as Milan-Bergamo, Orio al Serio and Il Caravaggio International Airport) is situated 45km Northeast of Milan. It's a huge base for Ryanair, which has flights to cities in the UK, Italy, all over Europe and even the Middle East and North Africa. However, it's less convenient for Ticino than Malpensa: although there are some direct buses to Lugano (run by Flixbus; www.flixbus.co.uk) they are infrequent and take just over two and a half hours to make the journey. You are far more likely to end up taking one of the frequent buses from the airport to Milano Centrale rail station and then taking a train into Ticino (1 hr 15 min to Lugano, 1 hr 35 min to Bellinzona). Milan's third airport, which is only 7km from the city centre, is Linate; British Airways, Aer Lingus, Easyjet and the Italian national carrier ITA (formerly Alitalia) operate flights from there to the UK and Ireland. There are buses from the airport to Centrale station but no direct buses to Ticino.

Zurich and Lugano airports

Zurich is Switzerland's major international airport, with flights all over the world. It takes around 2 hr 10 min to reach Lugano by train from the airport's railway station, with at least one change. It's not quite as convenient as Malpensa unless you are heading for the north of Ticino, as travelling times from Zurich airport to Airolo (2 hr 15 min) are slightly less than they are to there from Malpensa (around 3 hr 40 min). Ticino's only civilian airport serves Lugano and is situated at Agno, west of the city. In the past only a few scheduled flights have operated from here, mainly to destinations in Switzerland and Italy; however, following the reduction in air travel caused by the Covid-19 pandemic, the airport's long-term future was unclear at the time of writing.

LOCAL TRANSPORT AND DRIVING

Switzerland's extraordinary public transport system is a blessing for walkers. Fast, frequent and comfortable trains whisk you between the various centres in Ticino, which are then linked to even the smallest hamlets by a dense network of rural buses: many of the walks in this book take advantage of this, beginning at one bus stop and ending at another – indeed all walks in this book have been explicitly structured around public transport access at either end.

Most places offering accommodation in Ticino provide their guests with a Ticino Ticket (or Ticino card) which offers unlimited use of all buses and trains in the canton up until midnight of the day of departure; a number of discounts (at museums, on mountain transport and on tourist boats on Lakes Lugano and Maggiore, and at other attractions) are also offered to those holding the card (details on www.ticino.ch/en/ticket). You can't buy this ticket – it is issued to guests as they check in to their accommodation – and such is its value and versatility that it's worth checking with your accommodation provider before booking that they offer it to their guests, as holders save a huge amount of both money and time (buying tickets from bus drivers or machines at railway stations each time you make a journey is something of a hassle). Tickets (available in paper form or as digital downloads on a smartphone) have your name on them and are not valid unless you also have an identity document with you (probably your passport).

Those who are planning to travel in other parts of Switzerland might be interested in purchasing the Swiss Travel Pass, which offers unlimited travel on boats, trains and buses throughout the country for either a number of consecutive days, or for a number of freely selectable days within a month; the pass also offers reductions on mountain transport fares and entrance to museums and other attractions. For more information see the website of Swiss Federal Railways, www.sbb.ch.

This website can also be used for timetables and route planning; it's a dream to use and includes bus services as well as trains, detailing clearly when you need to use both forms of transport for any journey. This timetable does not, however, include boats on Lakes Lugano and Maggiore, or mountain transport.

Trains

Switzerland is known worldwide for its trains, operated by Swiss Federal Railways (Schweizerische Bundesbahnen or SBB in German; Ferrovie Federali Svizzere or FFS in Italian). The main line through Ticino links Chiasso right in the south of the Canton to Airolo in the north, via Lugano, Bellinzona, Biasca and Faido; there are hourly or half-hourly local trains along this route throughout the day, while express trains also link Bellinzona with Lugano and Chiasso, not stopping at intermediate stations (many of these are international trains running from Milan to Zurich). North of Biasca fast trains plunge into the

The Centovalli line, seen here at Intragna just west of Locarno, is one of the most scenic in Ticino

mountains via the new Gotthard Base Tunnel (which opened in December 2016), emerging some 35 miles to the north at Erstfeld in Canton Uri; at 57km (35 miles) this is the longest, and also the deepest, rail tunnel in the world. Local trains heading north enter the older, shorter Gotthard Tunnel at Airolo, emerging in Canton Uri at Göschenen and eventually terminating at Erstfeld.

Other lines are the short branch to Locarno (with some direct trains from Lugano – otherwise, change at Giubiasco or Bellinzona for the 25-minute journey), the narrow gauge Centovalli rail line from Locarno to Domodossola in Italy (see Walk 13) and a little-used line that runs from Giubiasco into Italy via the eastern shore of Lake Maggiore.

Local train services are run by a cross-border concern, TILO (Treni regionali Ticino Lombardia; www.tilo. ch) with many services in Ticino continuing on across the border to Como, Milan and Malpensa Airport (see Malpensa airport in the introduction).

Buses

Yellow postbuses emblazoned with the image of a horn are a familiar sight all over Ticino. They are mostly operated by Postbus Switzerland, a subsidiary company of the Swiss Post Office, though in some areas the services are run by private companies (such as Autolinee Bleniesi in the Val Blenio).

Postbuses, like this one at Fusio, at the start of walk 15, are the main way of accessing the walks described in this book (photo: NAC, Wikimedia Commons)

Services generally depart from out-side railway stations (Lugano is the exception to this rule, where separate regional and local bus stations can be found some distance from the train station). On rural routes (with narrow roads) minibuses are often used rather than standard coaches. These routes may have only a couple of services each day; on many routes, however, services are hourly. Note that some bus routes (particularly those over mountain passes) only operate from late spring to early autumn (dates vary with each route).

Mountain transport

Many walks in this book are accessed by mountain transport – mainly cable cars but also funicular railways and chairlifts.

Cable cars or gondolas (*funivia* in Italian) are cabins suspended from cables that glide effortlessly up the often precipitously steep sides of val-leys; cabins either hold 4 or 6 passen-gers, such as the ones up to Tremorgio for Walks 36 and 38, or Mornera for Walk 24, or they are much bigger, holding dozens of people in one go – such as the ones at Robiei (for Walk 16) or Airolo (for Walks 33 and 36). Chairlifts, such as the one up Pian Nara used to access Walk 28, are similar but comprise uncovered chairs rather than cabins.

Funicular railways (*funicolare* in Italian) are cabins that run on rails, hauled up by cables. In Lugano a funicular links the train station with the town centre, forming part of the city's municipal public transport system. However, the most important funiculars in Ticino for walkers are those linking Paradiso with Monte San Salvatore (for Walk 3) and linking Piotta with Piora (for Walk 37).

Beware that many forms of mountain transport only operate from late spring to early autumn, or even just during high summer – precise dates vary with each operator, and be warned that operations may not be daily, even in July and August. It always pays to check in advance via websites whether the funicular or cable car you need to access your walk is operational.

Also note that cable cars can close down for months (or even years) for maintenance and that at busy times there may be queues to get on – booking in advance via websites is eminently sensible, for instance, on Saturday or Sunday mornings of fine days in July or August. Also note that some cable cars and chairlifts only operate in winter, when they give access to skiing grounds – and so are useless for walkers – and that even if a cable car closes it can still remain marked on maps years later (another reason for checking in advance that a cable car you want to use is actually operational). Some cable cars marked on maps are also privately owned and only carry freight – and so can't be used to plan walks around.

Driving

Driving to walking start-points means that you are unconstrained by bus and train timetables – and although many of the walks in this book are linear, there will always be straightforward public transport that allows you to get back to your car. Car rental is expensive – it's best arranged in advance, online – and if you are renting a car from one of the North Italian airports make sure you can drive it across the border.

Your own national driving licence or an international drivers' licence is needed to drive in Switzerland. Speed limits are 120kph on motorways, 80kph on main roads (100kph on routes designated *semi-autostrade*) and 50kph in urban areas (although watch out for 30kph or 20kph limits on some streets). At junctions, yellow diamonds painted on the road show who has priority, while on gradients vehicles heading uphill always have priority; if in doubt, give way to traffic coming from the right – and to all buses. Postbuses always have priority and make their presence known on narrow, twisting mountain roads via a loud hoot on their horn.

Parking can be limited and prohibitively expensive – when choosing accommodation always make sure you can park your car outside. Covered parking garages are signposted in cities, and are very expensive. Elsewhere, parking is controlled by colour-coded zones: white lines denote that parking can be paid for via a central paypoint or individual meters (pay with coins or via an app – either put your numberplate or the number of your space into the machine, or collect a ticket to display); blue zones and red zones require a special disc, often included in the glove box of rental cars or available from tourist offices, police stations, banks and car rental agencies. The blue discs require the time to be set via a dial while the red disc gives 15 hours of free parking. Yellow-marked zones are privately owned spaces used by suppliers of nearby shops and offices – where parking is forbidden.

INFORMATION AND MAPS

Switzerland more or less invented modern tourism (in the way we would understand it today) and not surprisingly it has a very comprehensive tourist infrastructure. There are tourist offices in most large towns (often located in the railway station) where the staff will speak English and will be knowledgeable about local walks – though be warned that most tourist offices close for an hour or two for lunch and are shut on Sunday. The website of the canton's tourism agency is also crammed full of information and recommendations (www.ticino.ch).

Red and white track markers show walkers the way – these are on the trail through the Val di Campo on Walk 29

Tourist offices (along with bookshops, hotel receptions and the kiosks attached to railway stations) are also the best places to buy maps. As you might expect, the country is comprehensively and accurately mapped, and a fold-out printed map is vital for any walk (don't rely on maps viewable by mobile phone, which are less versatile when viewed on a small screen, and also depend on your phone maintaining its battery charge for the whole length of the walk). The series of 1:25,000 fold-out maps with brown covers are unbeatable for their detail, though less detailed maps (with green covers) are also available at 1:50,000 scale. Both are great for hiking and both are published by the Bundesamt für Landestopografie (Swiss Federal Office of Topography or 'Swisstopo'). Eighteen individual maps in the 1:25,000 series and eight individual maps in the 1:50,000 series cover Ticino – check carefully the area covered by each map before you buy one. In addition, there are other standalone hiking maps for individual regions within Ticino, published by independent publishers (though using Swisstopo cartographic data).

Unfortunately, all these maps are rather expensive to purchase; there seems to be no way around this, though always ask at tourist offices if they have free maps – sometimes these are too basic for hiking purposes, though on occasions the free maps offered by tourist offices can be as detailed as a purchased map, so it's always worth asking. The best online map of Switzerland is available at www.map.geo.admin.ch/ – you can zoom in and out with ease, and the level of on-screen detail is astonishing.

WEATHER AND WHEN TO VISIT

Ticino's climate is generally mild, with rain all year round. Most locations receive 1500–1900mm of rain annually (it gets wetter the higher and further north you go – and figures are lower than this south of Lugano). This is around the same total as much of the English Pennines or the lower parts of the West Highlands of Scotland. Temperatures are subject to extremes – the very highest mountains are snowcapped all year round, but on sunny afternoons in mid-summer it can get uncomfortably hot in the southern parts of Ticino. The Canton's climate is often described as 'Mediterranean' and although the wild fragrances and the brilliant sunlight are strongly reminiscent of Italy or the South of France, in reality Ticino is much rainier than most places around the Mediterranean (and the region has much wetter summers, in particular). The most significant aspect of the weather that walkers need to take heed of (apart from the rain) is that Ticino is the most lightning-prone part of Europe, with severe thunderstorms a common occurrence throughout the summer.

As in any mountain area, weather conditions can change rapidly and you should always be prepared for the temperature to drop and for rain clouds to bubble up: even mountain areas as apparently benign as Ticino can be dangerous places and they need to be treated with respect and caution. The weather can also be extremely localized, with blazing sunshine in one valley while rain is falling in the next. The forecasts provided by www.meteocentrale.ch or www.meteoswiss.admin.ch are usually accurate; you can search for towns and villages and it's usually safe to assume that the forecast available at breakfast time is a good indicator as to how the weather will unfold for the day. In the mountains, the most reliable weather forecasts are often those produced by the guardians of mountain huts, who infuse their forecasts with a wealth of local knowledge.

A more detailed month-by-month breakdown of the weather – and suggestions as to the best time to walk in Ticino – is as follows:

January–April
Skiers take to the slopes in Airolo and the Val Blenio and snow can fall anywhere – though is less likely around the lakes in the South, where some walks such as 1, 2 and 10 will probably remain open. By April the snow below 1200m should have melted and the gradually warming weather will tempt out the first walkers into the hills.

May and June
While snow may linger at around 1600m and above until June, many paths will now be open – though take care approaching the snowline as avalanches are not uncommon and can kill. At lower levels, wild flowers are at their glorious best at this time, the weather is sunny and warm, visibility is excellent with no heat haze, and the scenery is at its most photogenic, with some peaks still frosted with snow. Most cable cars start operating for the Summer in June and mountain passes begin to open to road traffic – and with the summer crowds still yet to descend this can be an excellent time to visit Ticino.

July and August
This is the height of the tourist season in Ticino, with warm weather and festivals in the cities (the Lugano Jazz Festival and the Locarno Film Festival) encouraging visitors in their droves. However, everywhere is busy, accommodation prices are at their highest, and the heat can bring on storms – it's best to visit in spring or early autumn if you can. Be aware that above 2400m there will still be patches of un-melted snow, even in late summer.

September
In many ways this is the ideal month to walk in Ticino. The heat and the storms of high summer have dissipated and the crowds have gone home, but the weather is still warm,

all paths are still open and most of the cable cars are still running.

October

The thickly wooded Ticino valleys can look lovely in autumn sunlight and there is still some fine walking to be done. However, most cable cars shut down in October for the winter, and bus services over mountain passes cease; walkers at high altitudes can experience cold temperatures and the weather can turn distinctly gloomy if clouds and rain set in.

November and December

November is the slackest month in Switzerland as far as tourism is concerned – it's too early for skiers and too rainy and cold for walkers. Many hoteliers shut up shop and go on holiday for the month; those that remain in business slash their prices. The weather can be as dreary and grey as anywhere else in Europe at this time – though on the occasional sunny days it's warm enough (just) to sit outside for lunch. Walkers now become restricted to only the lowest altitude routes in the south of the Canton – a situation that may persist well into March.

ACCOMMODATION

Many types of accommodation are available throughout Ticino. Unfortunately, Swiss accommodation

The village of Prato, which Walk 15 passes through

25

Bignasco, at the end of Walk 15

is relatively expensive but for the money you pay you can always expect high standards, conscientious management and good service. Unfortunately, too, much of the accommodation is rather bland in terms of character – though the view from the window often more than makes up for this! Ticino is busy with tourists for much of the year, and in summer it can be positively heaving – so booking in advance is strongly advised. If you arrive somewhere with nowhere to stay then tourist offices keep lists of accommodation and may help you with booking – or use the courtesy phones found at their offices or at railway stations. If you are driving to a hotel, look out for the yellow-and-brown signposts that direct drivers to hotels from town centres and outskirts. Before arranging any accommodation it's worthwhile enquiring in advance whether they provide guests with a Ticino Ticket (see above), which allows for free use of public transport and discounts on local attractions. Note that in some places you will have to pay a small local tax of a few Francs on top of the accommodation cost, which will need to be paid in cash when you leave and will not have been included in advance payments if you have pre-booked.

Hotels

Hotels are always comfortable, clean and respectable – though vary hugely in price: luxury waterside palaces with balconies and views of a lake can charge eye-wateringly high prices, whereas smaller hotels beside a main road in a small, non-touristy town or suburb will of course be much more reasonably priced. Often these cheaper hotels call themselves *garni* which means that they do not offer lunch or dinner – only breakfast. Some older hotels still offer rooms without en-suite facilities: the bathroom will be along the corridor. If you don't mind this, you can save a lot of money opting for this category of room.

Guesthouses

Often cheaper than hotels are guesthouses (*albergo*) and *ristorante con alloggio* (literally 'restaurants with rooms') – both of which normally comprise a group of guest bedrooms (en-suite and not en-suite) situated above or adjacent to a restaurant. These family-owned places tend (like the cheaper hotels) to be situated on main roads in non-touristy towns, villages or suburbs; they are often rather ordinary in ambience – don't expect a lakes-and-mountains view from the window – but they are inevitably clean, and prices, like the rooms themselves, are modest. Some of these places are listed on accommodation-booking websites, while others can be found after a straightforward internet search; advance reservation will probably need to be made by phone or email.

Youth hostels

There are three Hostelling International affiliated hostels (*ostello della gioventù* in Italian) in Ticino – in suburban districts of Lugano, Bellinzona and Locarno. They are very popular with walkers and are discussed in the relevant introductory sections of each chapter in this book. Accommodation in each includes dormitory beds along with doubles and singles – some en-suite, some not. Booking and checking prices and availability is very easy on the Swiss Youth Hostels website (www. youthhostel.ch). Hostels also offer very reasonably priced meals to overnight guests – worth remembering as eating out in Switzerland is expensive. Swiss Backpackers (www.swisshostels.com) is a rival group of independent hostels which are a bit less institutional than Swiss Youth Hostels – their two Ticino hostels are in fairly remote locations outside Locarno.

Bed and breakfasts and private rooms

Bed and breakfast accommodation involves lodging in someone's private home; there are usually several rooms on offer, some en-suite, some not. Breakfast will always be provided and many places will also provide an evening meal (at a cost, and arranged each day in advance). Expect to pay 50–70 Francs per night – more for better-appointed properties with fine views or lakeside locations. The website www.bnb.ch shows all the possibilities – everything from in-the-middle-of-nowhere chalets to city townhouses are on offer. Reservations need to be made by emailing the establishment directly; when it comes to payment this will usually need to be made in cash.

There are also hundreds of accommodation options in private homes offered via the accommodation booking service www.airbnb.co.uk. These tend to be concentrated in resort towns rather than the countryside; living arrangements are more informal than the traditional bed and breakfasts and are unlikely to include prepared meals.

In Ticino you can also arrange accommodation with private providers on the spot – in villages look out for the words *affitasi camere* (or the German *zimmer frei*) which indicates rooms for rent in private houses; payment for these will again need to be made in cash.

Chalets

Renting a chalet means you will get the whole run of the house or apartment – including the use of the pool, if there is one (the owners of the property won't be there). This makes these places particularly appropriate for families or large groups. High season bookings are often for a minimum of seven nights. One of the biggest agencies offering chalets is interhome (www.interhome.com/switzerland/ticino/). They have hundreds of options on their website, including some in-the-middle-of-nowhere options that will appeal to walkers. General accommodation websites such as www.expedia.co.uk also offer a variety of chalet accommodation.

The village of Morcote, at the end of Walk 3

Camping

There are over thirty official campsites in Ticino – though they tend to be concentrated around the lakes in the south rather than in mountain areas to the north. All are listed on www.camping. info, which allows a comprehensive search to be made on each site regarding location, facilities and prices. Some of the larger sites offer cabins, bungalows, apartments or caravans for rent alongside space for pitching tents – and these tend to be the sites which also offer facilities such as swimming pools, private beaches (on the lakes), bike hire, kids' playgrounds, supermarkets, restaurants and the like. If you're after one of these sites (which also tend to stay open all year rather than have a winter closure period), take a look at Muzzano (on Lake Lugano) and Campofelice, Camping Tamaro and Lido Mappo (all on the shores of Lake Maggiore). Wild camping is only allowed in the mountains above the treeline, and is forbidden in nature reserves and certain other areas; always contact local authorities in advance to check where camping is allowed – and remember to clean up after yourself.

Farm stays

A number of farms throughout Switzerland have opened their doors to 'agritourism' – where guests stay in basic accommodation on a farm, often being able to view (or even participate in) farm activities (such as viticulture or animal husbandry). Many farms offer B&B-style rooms, but a selling point of some is the option to 'sleep on straw' (*dormire sulla paglia* or *schlaf im Stroh* in German) which is what it says it is – you simply place your sleeping bag on a bed of straw. Most accommodation of this kind is available only from May to October and sleeps only a few people (maybe 10–15), making it particularly appealing to families. Both types of farm stay also offer guests outdoor activities such as horse riding or even canoeing or volleyball. What is on offer at each farm is different – to search the possibilities, visit https:// farm.myswitzerland.com/en, www. agriturismo.ch or www.bauernhof-ferien.ch (properties listed on the latter tend to be more of the B&B type); bookings are normally made directly with each proprietor.

Accommodation in the mountains

Many of the walks in this book make use of mountain huts (*capanna*) run by CAS (Club Alpino Svizzero; www. casticino.ch/) or by UTOE (L'Unione Ticinese Operai Escursionisti; www. utoe.ch). Situated in spectacular locations that are usually inaccessible by road, most huts are based around traditional, formerly agricultural buildings that have modern extensions – though a few more modern Ticino huts have been purpose-built from scratch. During the day the huts will offer snacks and basic meals to hungry walkers, while during the night they offer dormitory

The Capanna Leit, the destination of walkers on Walk 38, is one of the more modern capannas; like all capannas it provides meals and accommodation

accommodation, allowing walkers to engage in hikes that last two days or more. Reservation in advance is usually possible by phone or online; the huts will provide an evening meal and breakfast and it can be an exhilarating experience waking up in such a place for a day's walking in high mountain countryside.

Be warned, however, that huts can close for months (or even years) for renovation work – always phone ahead if you intend to stay in (or even just visit) one of these huts. Some huts close during the winter – if there's no warden present, however, they are often left open, so walkers can seek shelter or obtain refreshments (the latter via an honesty box system). In addition, it's worth bearing in mind that staying at these huts can be relatively expensive – though this reflects the fact that the buildings are expensive to construct and maintain and that supplies must be brought in by helicopter. Cashless payments are accepted in many huts, though you should always have enough cash on you just in case – and bear in mind that the mobile phone signal may be weak (or non-existent) and that many huts have no wi-fi or phone-charging facilities.

A *rifugio* (refuge) is different to a *capanna*: rarely is a custodian present and if you turn up on spec you may well find the place locked and deserted. Accommodation will only be for a few people and there will be no meals provided: instead there will be basic kitchen facilities where you can prepare your own food. If you wish to stay at a *rifugio* find the contact details for the custodian via an internet search, and email in advance to enquire about prices, availability and facilities.

FOOD AND DRINK

Not surprisingly, Ticino's cuisine is firmly rooted in Italian traditions: you can get a pizza or a dish of pasta almost anywhere, though if you want something more authentically Ticinese, here are some dishes to try – perhaps in a *grotto*, a restaurant with a more traditional or rustic atmosphere than the local pizzeria. (Note that eateries in out-of-the-way places are usually closed for one or possibly even two days a week – usually Monday, Tuesday or Wednesday.)

Local minestrone soup is made from a blend of potatoes, beans, rice, tomatoes, leeks, carrots, cauliflower, peas and any other vegetables, with homemade pasta and local sbrinz cheese (similar to Italian parmesan) completing the picture.

Polenta – a North Italian staple, made from boiled maize – has a long tradition in Ticino and has been a basic food for a significant part of the population for centuries. Some *grotti* still prepare polenta in the traditional way, cooked for a long period over a crackling fire.

Saffron risotto is a creamy Ticino specialty, made with Swiss saffron that is grown in the canton of Valais, along with rice, butter, onions, garlic, tomatoes, meat stock, and meats such as veal and bacon; it is often seasoned with thyme, salt, and pepper.

You'll need something to wash all this down with – and the ideal choice is the local Merlot wine, grown in vineyards in the south of the canton around Mendrisio, Bellinzona and Lugano. Merlot (mostly red, though white merlot wine is also produced) accounts for 80 per cent of Ticino wine production; other wines produced in the canton include Pinot Noir, Riesling and Chardonnay – along with grappa, a strong, grape-based brandy. Local beers include a number of craft beers; one is the splendidly-named Bad Attitude, brewed in Stabio near Mendrisio.

In terms of where to buy food, there are traditional fresh-produce shops in a number of places but most walkers make good use of the well-stocked supermarkets in major towns – the Migros chain predominates, with Co-op and the discount chain Denner giving them a run for their money in terms of competition. Many supermarkets are shut on Sunday and also close for an hour or two around midday; stores with longer opening hours can be found at main railway stations. Many villages (and even some small towns) have no retail outlets at all, which often comes as a surprise for hungry and thirsty walkers.

A fresh produce store in Ascona

Locally-sourced food is available from outdoor markets, where farmers and producers sell their wares direct to the public. One of the best is in Bellinzona (Saturdays year-round 7.30am–1pm, with a smaller version operating 10am–5pm on Wednesdays in early summer, early autumn and during December); other large markets include Lugano (Tuesday and Fridays 7.30am–2pm), Locarno (Wednesday and Thursday 9am–5pm), Mendrisio (Wednesdays 9am–2pm) and Chiasso (Fridays 8am–5pm). The most famous outdoor market in the region is the Wednesday market in Luino on the Italian shores of Lake Maggiore (35 minutes by train from Cadenazzo on the Bellinzona–Locarno line).

WHAT TO TAKE

Not having the right equipment when out in the mountains can make a walk uncomfortable, unpleasant or even dangerous. It makes sense to be adequately equipped for the worst weather and for the most difficult terrain you will encounter; that said, a number of the walks in this book do not take you very high and stick reasonably close to settlement, which will be useful should the weather turn nasty. This means you should tailor what you take on a walk accordingly. Weight is also worth taking into account – too little and you might be ill-equipped, too much and you may find yourself struggling on the ascents.

Boots should be good quality, should fit comfortably and should be worn in before you set off for Switzerland. They should have good ankle support and thick cleated soles (such as Vibram). However, on low valley walks along woodland paths a pair of stout trainers should be adequate – except after rain, when muddy stretches and some standing water can render trainers inadequate.

Good-quality walking socks are also recommended. They should fit properly and be quick-drying – for all those times you end up crossing boggy patches of ground.

A good-quality waterproof jacket made from breathable fabrics is vital; even if the forecast is for dry weather, sudden storms can always blow in, and a jacket will be warm as well as waterproof. Many walkers also carry a pair of waterproof trousers.

Most walkers know about the important of layering. A base layer will draw moisture outwards from your body, while a fleece will act as a mid-layer and your jacket will act as an outer layer. Many people walk in shorts during the summer though it's no fun to walk on narrow paths through dense prickly foliage in shorts, so always bring a pair of long trousers with you if you choose to do this: they will also be useful for the occasions when a breeze springs up without warning (winds can be surprisingly cold at altitude) or the sun goes in and the temperature drops suddenly. A hat and gloves will also

be important. One thing to consider before setting off is how much of a change in altitude your walk will entail: on fine summer days it can be warm at the start of your walk in the valley floor, but the temperature will drop as you ascend – and then rise again as you descend into the baking valley floor in the late afternoon.

Rucksacks should have well-padded shoulder straps and waistband and should sit on your hips rather than your shoulders. A waterproof liner is a good investment; alternatively, put anything you wish to keep dry in a waterproof bag.

Walking Poles transfer some of the weight from your legs onto your arms and are vital if you are walking at altitude and encounter snow patches. On descents they can reduce the likelihood of falling or twisting your ankle. You will find that most walkers in Ticino use them on the rockier, high-altitude paths.

Other things to bring include a first aid kit, a small torch (flashlight) with spare batteries, a whistle for emergencies, and a space blanket or emergency bag which are light and could save someone's life.

Always carry a map and compass and know how to use them – electronic GPS devices are no substitute and can fail; if you are carrying one bring along spare batteries.

Sunscreen, sunglasses, lip salve and a sun hat (with a brim) are vital in summer, to cope with dazzling sun and unshaded heat – and you should also carry at least 1.5 litres of water per person (natural water courses should be treated with caution as a potential source of drinking water as livestock might be grazing near them, though hewn-out troughs found in valley pastures, which are filled by spring-fed pipes, should be perfectly safe to drink from).

WALKING PRACTICALITIES

In many respects Ticino is a very easy area to walk in. One reason for this is the quality of signage and the marking of tracks. Paths have developed over the centuries by farmers and hunters going about their daily business – from alp (area of high pastureland) to alp, or from valley to valley across an ancient pass, or up to a ridge where chamois can be spotted. Other paths are historic trading routes or mule trails that have been in existence for generations. Only a few paths are more recent, having been made by local communes, or by local agencies engaged in the management of footpaths, or by a climbing association to give access to their hut. In some places steep slopes are tackled by flights of steps made out of natural flagstones cut into the hillsides. Elsewhere, however, paths may have fallen into disuse, and a path shown on a map should not be taken as proof of existence of a trail on the ground.

Track junctions are clearly indicated by yellow signs on poles (or occasionally affixed to rocks or the side of buildings), detailing walking routes and timings (the latter are given in *ora* [hours] and *min* [minutes]). Destinations listed on these signs include villages, towns, railway stations (usually indicated by the acronym FFS), bus stops, cable car stations (usually marked *funivia*), remote lakes, mountain summits, mountain huts and refuges, and other important track junctions. Beside some bus stops, country railway stations and cable car top stations there's a veritable forest of these signs! A white plate on the signs indicates the name of the immediate locality and often gives the altitude – useful if you are trying to find out where you are on a map.

On walks themselves, white and red track markers painted at regular intervals on trees, walls and rocks point out the path, though even in high mountain areas the way is usually obvious, the path being either well-trodden or well-maintained. (In higher areas there are also paths marked with blue and white markers, which are high-altitude trails for experienced walkers that may require some specialist equipment to navigate.) Be warned, however, that in some areas these painted markers can be faded or hard to spot.

Yellow diamonds with black borders, printed on small metal signs and affixed to trees, walls or buildings, are also used as an alternative to the red-and-white painted markers. These often point out a specific, named

The approach to Capanna Cristallina on Walk 16, one of the highest mountain huts, is via this wild valley

sentiero (path or route) that remains in the valley or which runs along a hillside at a moderate altitude (unless the path is specifically designated as a *sentiero di montagne*, in which case it will be rougher and go higher in altitude); such paths are usually very well maintained and graded. Whichever markers you are following, it's always a good idea to keep your eye out for them – if you haven't seen one for a couple of hundred metres you have probably strayed from the path. The vast majority of trails described in this book are along red-and-white marked paths and so are accessible to most fit and experienced walkers.

Do not stray from paths deliberately – not only might you get lost, you might end up in areas that are potentially dangerous (through being vulnerable to rock falls for example) and you will cause unnecessary erosion of slopes.

SAFETY IN THE MOUNTAINS

The Ticino countryside can seem a benign presence on a sunny day. However, a change in the weather or a twisted ankle can easily turn a pleasant day out into something life threatening. For this reason, mountains should be treated with respect and you should also learn and understand your own capabilities: it goes without saying that those who are in fair physical shape on their arrival

Resting up by a track marker post – this one is at Passo d'Agario on Walk 6

will gain most from a walking holiday (here or anywhere else). Don't make the mistake of taking on too much for the first day or so, but instead build up distance and height-gaining steadily, day by day.

Regarding safety in the mountains, it is recommended that walking descriptions are read in advance and that plans are made based on the capabilities of the weakest member of the group. However, you should always be wary: path conditions may have been altered by a storm, rockfall or avalanche since route descriptions were written. Solo walkers on high mountain paths should exercise particular caution as alerting authorities if there is a problem will be more

problematic. All walkers should exercise prudence and use common sense when judging a situation that calls for care. Never be too proud to turn back should you find that your chosen route takes longer than anticipated, or if it becomes difficult or dangerous. Always think ahead.

Weather forecasts should be consulted in advance and plans altered (mid-walk if necessary) if bad weather is forecast – it can be dangerous to be in high and exposed mountain environments during storms. If you are caught out during a thunderstorm, avoid exposed high ground, drop your walking poles and stay away from trees, overhanging rocks and metal structures (the generally accepted advice is to squat close to the ground with your hands on your knees and your head tucked between them – try to touch as little of the ground with your body as possible, and avoid lying down.).

If possible, try to start your walk early in the day, to avoid afternoon heat and storms, and always carry adequate maps, clothing, food, drink and clothing with you. Watch out for dangers and annoyances, including mountain bikers (who might whizz up behind you totally unnoticed) and animals (give herds of cows and goats a wide berth if possible: a stampede of cattle is rare but has been known, while goats and sheep can often have shepherds looking after them with dogs that will become aggressive if you stray too close).

In the unhappy event of an accident, stay calm and move the injured person to a safe place and administer first aid. Establish your precise location (through GPS co-ordinates if possible) and call for help using a mobile (the emergency number is 112). The international distress call is a series of six signals (blasts on a whistle or torch flashes after dark) spaced evenly over a minute, followed by one minute's pause, followed by the six signals repeated. The reply is three signals per minute, followed by a minute's pause.

You are advised to take out comprehensive travel insurance before leaving home – making sure you stipulate that you will be hiking in mountain areas. UK citizens are also advised to apply for and carry a UK Global Health Insurance Card (GHIC) which allows access to state-provided, medically necessary healthcare at a reduced cost (or sometimes for free) in Switzerland. The cards can be accessed via the NHS website (www. nhs.uk) and are gradually replacing the old European Health Insurance Cards (which remain valid until their expiry date). EU citizens resident in the UK can apply for a UK-issued EHIC.

USING THIS GUIDE

The walks described in this book are only a taste of the hundreds of possibilities available in this amazing region. Four geographical areas are covered and you could easily spend a week or more in each. Most routes can be shortened or lengthened to meet your needs. A route summary table is included in Appendix A as a useful aid for choosing a walk.

Grading of walks

The intention of this guide is that walkers of all degrees of commitment will find something of value contained within it. Grading is not an exact science and the three categories used will cover a fairly wide spectrum.

- **Grade 1:** Suitable for family outings. Short distances along (mostly) gently graded paths or tracks with little change in height. Any steep ascents or descents are short.

- **Grade 2:** Moderate walking on clear footpaths, with some altitude change; walkers need to be adequately equipped.
- **Grade 3:** More strenuous and often longer routes on rough paths with some scrambling in places and steep ascents and descents; walkers following these routes should be well equipped.

Timings
These indicate the time for a reasonably fit walker to complete a walk. They do not include any resting time.

Distances
Distances are measures in kilometres, to match the maps and signposts in Switzerland. Mile equivalents are given in the information boxes at the start of each walk description. One mile equates to 1.6km.

Total ascent and descent
The total ascent is the aggregate of all the altitude gain on the total uphill sections of the walk. Total descent is the aggregate of the height losses on the downhill sections. Ascent and descent are measured in metres. As a rule of thumb, a fit walker climbs 300–400m in an hour.

Maps
Each description includes a sketch map. These are indicative only and are no substitute for the detail on the

In the picturesque village of Curzútt, which Walk 21 passes through

The Chapel of San Bernardo, which Walk 21 passes

GPX tracks

GPX tracks for the routes in this guidebook are available to download free at www.cicerone.co.uk/1060/GPX. If you have not bought the book through the Cicerone website, or have bought the book without opening an account, please register your purchase in your Cicerone library to access GPX and update information.

A GPS device is an excellent aid to navigation, but you should also carry a map and compass and know how to use them. GPX files are provided in good faith, but in view of the profusion of formats and devices, neither the author nor the publisher accepts responsibility for their use. We provide files in a single standard GPX format that works on most devices and systems, but you may need to convert files to your preferred format using a GPX converter such as gpsvisualizer.com or one of the many other apps and online converters available.

recommended maps (see Information and maps). You are much less likely to get lost or take a wrong turning if you use the recommended maps in conjunction with the maps published in this guide.

GENERAL INFORMATION

Language

The official language is Swiss Italian, which is very similar to standard Italian, though it presents some differences to the Italian spoken in Italy due to the presence of French and German from which it has assimilated some words. Some Lombard dialects are still spoken in the valleys, while Bosco Gurin (Chapter Two) is a remote village whose inhabitants have spoken German since its foundation (see Walk 17). German is the language of tourism (and is important in business) though English is also widely spoken by those whose jobs mean that they have frequent contact with visitors.

Money
The Swiss Franc (CHF) is the currency; one Franc (Fr; *Franco* in Italian) is divided into 100 *centesimi* (ct). Banks are everywhere (as you might expect) though ATM machines are not as ubiquitous as in some countries – there's normally one at railway stations. Most places accept payment using chip-and-pin cards, but beware that there are always exceptions that don't – including, most importantly, mountain huts, where often only cash is acceptable as payment.

Passports and visas
Despite not being in the EU Switzerland is a signatory to the Schengen agreement – which means those who need a visa must purchase one for all Schengen countries rather than for Switzerland specifically. European, American, Canadian, Australian and New Zealand passport holders do not need visas for Schengen agreement countries and need just their passport to enter the Schengen area; for other countries see www.schengenvisainfo.com.

Mobile phones
Mobile phones should work in towns and villages but in the mountains the signal is unreliable. 4G services are widely available so access to the internet from smartphones is usually possible.

International dialling code
The country code for Switzerland is +41; the first 0 of the area code is omitted if calling from outside the country.

Internet
Wi-fi is pretty standard in hotels, though in hostels and B&Bs it may only cover public areas, not bedrooms – check in advance if wi-fi availability is important to you. Some hotels provide a computer (with attached printer) for guests to use in their lobby. There are often no internet facilities in mountain huts or refuges.

Insurance
Mountain rescue services are unlikely to be free and you would be wise to take out adequate insurance that covers hiking. One specialist company that provides insurance for hikers is the British Mountaineering Council (www.thebmc.co.uk).

Emergencies
The emergency telephone number is 112.

Setting out for the summit of Monte Tamaro from the cable car station at Alpe Foppa (Walk 6)

WALKS FROM LUGANO

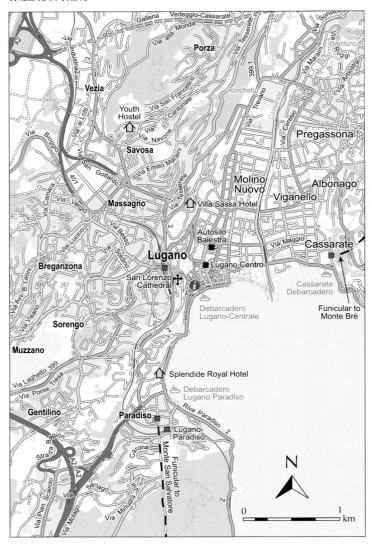

Caprino, one of the villages passed through on Walk 2

WALKS FROM LUGANO

Lugano, with a population of over 60,000 (and with over 150,000 living in its wider urban area), is by far the biggest settlement in Ticino; it's also the ninth biggest city in Switzerland and the biggest city outside Italy with a majority Italian-speaking population. The city's setting amidst the low, rounded peaks of the Pre-Alps, which overshadow the multiple curling arms of Lake Lugano (known also by its Latin name, *Ceresio*), is breathtaking – and with the station on a high ledge overlooking the town centre, this is surely one of the most exhilarating places on earth to arrive at by train.

The city is a major centre for banking, culture and light industry, but it's the lake that most visitors have come to see. The handsome city centre, with its Italianate piazzas and stylish boutiques, opens out onto the lake's long, palm-fringed promenade, ideal for the Italian tradition of *passegiata* – the evening stroll after a hot day. Through the day in summer boats depart from Lugano's landing stages bound for the smaller settlements that dot the lake's shore – some

43

of which, at the end of the lake's eastern and western arms, actually lie in Italy, with the international border drawn across the water.

Two funicular railways lie at either ends of the long promenade, one ascending to Monte Brè, the other to Monte San Salvatore (whose upper station is the start of walk 3). First-time visitors to Lugano might well want to use these jaunts as a way of getting their bearings and appreciating the city's stunning situation. In terms of what there is to see in Lugano itself, the city's major rainy-day attractions are actually covered in walk 1, and take the form of a series of galleries, museums and Baroque churches that line the waterfront – though don't overlook the Catedrale San Lorenzo, the city's

cathedral, which overlooks the town from an eyrie just down from the station.

WALKS ACCESSED FROM LUGANO

The walks in this chapter can be divided into three sections – those that hug the lake shore, those that ascend minor peaks that overlook the lake's shoreline, and longer walks in the mountain hinterland to the north of Lugano.

The first two walks are along the eastern arm of the lake; the first hugs the northern shore, terminating at the picturesque village of Gandria, while the second is along the southern shore, which is rather wilder, terminating at Cantine di Gandria. Both walks are very easy and straightforward and will probably be accessible all year. The first walk also passes many of Lugano's historical and cultural attractions, and both offer plenty of opportunity to pause for refreshment breaks at lakeside cafes and restaurants.

Gradients are a little harder in the next three walks, which ascend peaks whose lower slopes rise right from the lake shore, namely Monte San Salvatore (Walk 3), Monte Caslano (Walk 4) and Monte San Giorgio (Walk 5). The first of these walks is the longest, though has no appreciable uphill sections (as Monte San Salvatore is reached by funicular). All allow for spectacular vistas over the lake from the main viewpoints and the paths accessing them, all of which run through peaceful forests. Again, the walks should be accessible all year.

Lugano's hinterland to the north consists of high, treeless and often steep hills, which are explored in the remaining four walks in this chapter. These longer and more challenging routes still provide tantalizing views of the distant, shimmering lake, even if they are really mountain walks first and foremost. Premier among these is the 'classic' walk from Monte Tamaro to Monte Lema, one of the most trodden in the canton, whose starting and finishing points are accessed by cable cars. This is also the highest walk in this chapter, rising to an altitude of 1962m at the summit of Monte Tamaro.

The other walks rise to the summits of the highest peaks that overlook Lugano, namely Monte Bar and Monte Boglia, with routes beginning at the edge of Lugano's built-up area. The summits of these peaks provide for wonderful panoramic views over the lake and the city – and beyond, towards the plains of Northern Italy. The walk to Monte Boglia also continues on for an up-close encounter with some spectacular limestone pinnacles, and all three walks make use of *capannas*, isolated mountain huts in the hills that offer refreshments.

The final walk is the furthest from Lugano and explores the hilly ridges that divides the city and its region from Locarno and Bellinzona to the north, rising to the summit of Cima di Medeglia and making use of a former military road built a century ago by the Swiss army. Expect these higher walks to be closed by snow during the winter (indeed the Monte Tamaro walk may not be accessible until late June).

ACCOMMODATION

Although there's accommodation to be found in hotels and B&Bs in many lakeside villages such as Morcote (see Walk 3), Caslano (see Walk 4) and Campione d'Italia (see Walk 2), many walkers will want to base themselves in Lugano itself, which offers the most flexibility in terms of accessing as many walks as possible. The most expensive hotels are by the lake in the

centre of town and in Lugano's southern extension, Paradiso, which has its
own railway station. Opulence comes
in the form of the traditional, palatial
five-star hotels such as the Splendide
Royal by the waterside, or the more
contemporary Villa Sassa, a stylish
hideaway set away from the centre
on a hillside with fabulous views over
the town and lake. Hotels in the strag-
gle of rather ordinary suburbs that
stretch north from the centre towards
Cadempino and Taverne-Torricella are
rather more affordable – but you'll
have to get on a bus to get a view of
the water.

One of the most affordable
places to stay is Lugano's youth
hostel on Via Cantonale 13 in
Savosa (www.luganoyouthhostel.ch;
take bus #5 to Crocifisso from the
Genzana stop, 200m left from the
railway station). It may be situated
away from the lake shore in a residential suburb, but many city-centre
hotels would be proud to boast of
its palm-shaded gardens and open-
air swimming pool. There are also
a number of campsites around the
fringes of the city, such as the TCS
site at Lugano-Muzzano (www.tcs-
camping.ch), which has a waterside
location in Agno, the city's western
suburb; there's an on-site restaurant and shop, and you can also
rent cabins. Close by is a similar
site, Camping Lugano Lake (www.
campingluganolake.ch), while a
number of other sites dot both the
Swiss and Italian shores of the lake.

INFORMATION AND MAPS

The tourist office in Lugano (open
Mon–Sat 9am–noon and 1–6pm [5pm
Sat], Sun 10am–noon and 1–4pm;
www.luganoturismo.ch) is located on
the main square, the Piazza Riforma,
and offers a free map – Lugano Hiking
Map – that shows all the walking
routes described in this section (and
many other options to explore), albeit
at rather a small scale. In terms of
the 1:50,000 scale maps with hiking trails published in the Schweizer
Wanderweg series, map 286T
Malcantone includes all of the routes
described below. The 1:25,000 map
Bellinzona Gambarogno also covers
walks 6 and 9.

PUBLIC TRANSPORT

Mainline trains
Lugano is on the trunk rail route
through Ticino, with a mixture of
local and express trains running north
to Locarno and Bellinzona and on
through the Gotthard tunnels to central Switzerland, and south to Chiasso
(on the Italian border) and then Como
and Milan.

Ferrovia Lugano-Ponte Tresa
Narrow gauge FLP trains operate
from a station across the plaza from
the main station (and at a lower level)
to Ponte Tresa on the Italian border.
Walk 4 is accessed via this line.

Local buses

Lugano has an extensive local bus network (TPL, Trasporti Publicci Luganesi). The focus of the routes is the main local bus station Lugano Centro, 250m north of the main square, Piazza Riforma.

Regional buses

Buses in the Lugano region are operated by Autolinee Regionali Luganesi (ARL) and the Autopostale post bus service. The main bus station for these buses is the Autosilo Balestra located 500m north of the Piazza Riforma, though most buses can be caught in the centre of town or outside the station.

Boats on Lake Lugano

Tourist boat services on Lake Lugano (early-April to late-October only) are operated by SNL (www.lakelugano. ch). The main *debarcadero* (boat landing stage) is close to the Piazza Riforma in Lugano. Services run to all parts of the lake (including places on the Italian shores). A number of walks in this section begin or end at a *debarcadero*. Tickets can be quite expensive but there's a reduction if you use a Ticino Ticket (see Local transport and driving).

The view over Caslano enjoyed by walkers from the summit of Monte Caslano (Walk 4)

WALK 1
Lake Lugano shoreline from Paradiso to Gandria

Start	Paradiso *debarcadero*
Finish	Gandria *debarcadero*
Distance	6.25km (4 miles)
Ascent	40m
Descent	40m
Difficulty	Grade 1
Walking time	1 hr 45 min
Terrain	Paved surfaces underfoot the whole length of the walk, with minimal ascent and descent
Refreshments	There are bars and restaurants along most of the walk's length, and shops along the first part.

A walk like no other in this book, this route takes in the length of Lugano's gorgeous palm-fringed lakeside promenade, beginning in Paradiso, the city's southern extension, and ending in the carless and picturesque village of Gandria, which clings to the precipitous cliffs that girt the lake's eastern arm. Lugano is Ticino's main cultural centre and boasts a number of fine museums and galleries; this walk passes three of them, along with one of the city's finest churches. The second part of the walk runs along a purpose-built cliff-edge footpath, and while not exactly wild countryside, there's a definite feeling as you approach Gandria that Lugano's often tiresome crowds have been left far behind. Although this walk could really be described as an 'extended lakeside stroll' it's none the poorer for that, and of course it can be undertaken in all weathers.

ACCESS

Bus #2 runs from central Lugano, and the train station, to the Paradiso *debarcadero*; in addition, local trains running south from Lugano towards Chiasso stop at Paradiso station, from where it's a 5-min walk down to the *debarcadero*. In Gandria the #490 bus to Lugano (hourly) leaves from the parking area behind the San Viglio church: the walk passes right by the front door of the church – follow the terrace round. In addition, Lake Lugano's tourist boats make for a more satisfying – though inevitably more expensive – method of accessing both ends of this walk. Services to Paradiso are very frequent, and in high season Gandria is served by 9 daily boats from Lugano – though watch for the lengthy interval in services in the afternoon.

Set off N from the **debarcadero** at Paradiso along the tree-shaded shoreline promenade. To the L is the appropriately-named **Hotel Splendide**, whose ornate frontage is a splendid riot of balconies and terraces, and this is followed by the **Museo della Culture** (see boxed text for details of this and the other museums this walk passes). After another 5 min something resembling a ship's hull made out of polished grey-green stone looks as if it is about to launch itself into the water – this is the smart new **Lugano Arte e Cultura** (LAC), Lugano's premier art gallery and cultural venue.

The route passes through the waterside Parco Ciani in Lugano

The LAC is best admired from the promenade itself, where there's a pink granite monument to Franz Kafka set right by the water, amidst a small sculpture park. Next door to the LAC is the **Chiesa Santa Maria degli Angeli**, cool on a hot day and with some wonderful frescoes adorning its walls. On its north side is the disused trackbed of a funicular railway which closed in 1986; the flight of steps beside the trackbed gives access to a good viewpoint over the lake and city.

Beyond the Kafka monument the route continues along the promenade, curving round to the E and passing a fountain (behind which is Lugano's principal square, Piazza Riforma) and the city's two main boat landing stages. The promenade finally ends at the gates to a waterside garden, the **Parco Ciani**; pass through the gates and head on E along the shoreline path, in the shadow of the pastel-pink Villa Ciani. The modern buildings further on to your L are the cantonal library and, immediately beyond, the **Natural History Museum** (entrance to the latter is from the N or 'landward' side).

Paths divide outside the S side of the Natural History Museum. Take the one that hugs the south wall of the museum, which leads to a footbridge over the Cassarate river; once over the bridge turn N (L), along the Via Foce, and then R at a road junction along a main road, the Viale Castagnola. Some 10 min from the road junction you pass the **Vermouth by Martini** bar on the L, the last refreshment stop for a while, as it's at this point that the route begins to head out of Lugano's centre. ▶ From the bar it's another 10 min along the main road to the San Domenico bus stop. Here you should fork R along the Via Cortivo (look out for the yellow walking sign for Gandria).

There's an interesting variety of **residences** along the Via Cortivo, from ornate nineteenth century villas to stylish contemporary apartment blocks – all of course affording wonderful views over the lake, and all carrying an air of quiet exclusivity about them.

Beside the bar is the Via Funicolare, which leads to the base station of a funicular railway up Monte Brè, the sugarloaf mountain that looms over Lugano from the east.

51

After 10 min the Via Cortivo terminates in a small car park that gives access to a purpose-built footpath, the Sentiero di Gandria (aka the Sentiero d'Olivio), which clings picturesquely to a terrace just above the lake shore and passes through protected olive groves. After 10 min the path passes some public toilets; for the 15 min that follows the path enters a wilder stretch, ducking through some landslip protection arches before curling up and around an attractive cove. Once you drop down from the cove you'll find yourself in **Gandria**.

Gandria is an almost impossibly picturesque village of stone staircases, winding lanes, dark passageways and brightly-coloured window boxes, the

The lakeside village of Gandria, at the end of the walk

whole ensemble looking as if it might slide off the cliff and into the lake at any moment!

The path passes right by the **San Viglio church**, which is the village focal point; a couple of low-key shoreline bar-restaurants lie a minute or so further on, beside the *debarcadero*.

MUSEUMS ALONG THE ROUTE

This walk passes right by three of Lugano's museums. The Musei della Culture (open 11am–6pm daily except Tuesday; www.mcl.lugano.ch) concentrates on ethnographic artworks from Southeast Asia and Oceania; the LAC (open 11am–6pm Tue/Wed/Fri, 11am–8pm Thurs, 10am–6pm Sat and Sun; www.luganolac.ch) has a permanent collection of Swiss and international art and also stages temporary exhibitions; while the Natural History Museum (open 9am–noon and 2–5pm daily except Monday; free entry; www4.ti.ch/dt/da/mcsn/temi/mcsn/il-museo/il-museo) concentrates on the flora, fauna and geology of the Ticino region, with items well-displayed but unfortunately with no information in English.

WALK 2
Campione d'Italia to Cantine di Gandria

Start	Campione d'Italia *debarcadero*
Finish	Museo Dogane *debarcadero* at Cantine di Gandria
Distance	6.75km (4.25 miles)
Ascent	200m
Descent	200m
Difficulty	Grade 1
Walking time	2 hr 15 min
Terrain	Mostly forest paths with some metalled roads
Refreshments	The path passes right by a number of *grotti* (restaurants) though they are quite pricey. The only shops are in Campione.

Complementing Walk 1, which runs east from Lugano along the north shore of the lake to Gandria, this walk follows the opposite shoreline, which is rocky, forested and much wilder. Beginning in Campione d'Italia, an uneven rectangle of Italian territory wholly surrounded by Switzerland, the walk rises up and over a steep promontory and then falls back down to hug the lake shoreline, affording magnificent views across to Lugano and Gandria along its entire length. Stops at the various waterside *grotti* along the route can easily turn the walk into a leisurely affair – and you can stretch it out to a long afternoon if you also factor in a look round the Customs Museum (Museo Dogane), where the walk terminates. Navigation is easy, and the walk can be done at any time of the year and in virtually all weathers.

ACCESS

Bus #439 runs from central Lugano to Campione (hourly or every two hours; 17 min). In Lugano the best place to pick it up is the stop by the waterfront fountain at Piazza Rezzonico; in Campione buses stop outside the enormous casino, 150m N of the *debarcadero*. There is no road access (so no bus) to Cantine di Gandria – at the end of your walk return the way you came, or cross to Lugano or Gandria by boat (see Walk 1 for how to reach Lugano from Gandria). Tourist boats make three daily crossings from Lugano to Campione (20 min). At Cantine there are two boat landing stages around 300m apart from one another (Museo Dogane and Cantine di Gandria), each with services to Lugano and Gandria (at different times).

Emerging from the **debarcadero** onto Campione's main piazza you'll see the first track marker post, which points the way E along a passageway squeezed between a restaurant and the branch of an (Italian) bank. The passageway, La Barchetta, takes you E then after 100m NE (as Via Bonino da Campione) to pass under Via Totone and onto Via Per Arogno, which in turn brings you to an upper section of Via Totone.

Crossing the Via Totone turn L along Via Per Arogno then immediately R up steps to rejoin the Via Per Arogno as it curves S then N around a harpin. After the hairpin turn L onto Via Pugerna, along which is a small parking

CAMPIONE D'ITALIA

Campione is an exclave – that is, a part of a country entirely surrounded by another – whose situation has resulted from historical accident: in 1512, when Pope Julius II transferred ownership of Ticino from the Bishop of Como to Switzerland, Campione stayed out of the arrangement, as it was the property of Milan's Abbey of Sant'Ambrogio. When Ticino chose to become a full part of the Swiss Confederation in 1798, the people of Campione opted to remain part of the Italian province of Lombardy (of which Milan is capital). Today Campione's most notable feature is its enormous casino, a stylish behemoth designed in 2007 by the Ticinese architect Mario Botta that takes advantage of the fact that Italy has more liberal gambling laws than Switzerland. The rest of the place largely consists of fairly ordinary apartment blocks, although there are some expensive hotels and restaurants scattered among them. Politically the place is a Swiss–Italian hybrid, its governance arrived at by numerous agreements between the two countries. Law and order, for instance, is in the hands of the Italian Carabinieri and Polizia Locale, but phoning here from Italy 'proper' means making an international call as Swisscom runs the telephone system. In terms of practicalities there are no passport checks, and the currency is the Swiss Franc (though Euros are widely accepted).

lot where a sign points the way L (N) to Caprino along a track that heads into the forest. (You're now 10 min from the *debarcadero*.)

After 10 min the path zig-zags up through the trees – the only serious ascent you'll do on this walk – and into open ground. Passing the final hairpin bend (marked by a bench) look L to see a sign marking the **border**, reading 'Svizzera 1921': this indicates that you are now back in Switzerland. After another 5 min (on minor roads) the route takes you through the hamlet of **Pügèrna**. Then it's down through trees to another equally quiet hamlet, **Bozze** (10 min from Pügèrna).

10 min beyond Bozze minor roads bring you to a path that drops down past a church, depositing you on another minor road that climbs up through the village of **Caprino**, a quiet place of secluded waterside villas. If the Osteria Caprino (L) with its outside terrace doesn't tempt you, turn R along the road and follow the marker

Caprino, one of the villages the walk passes through

posts onto a cobbled lane which then becomes another track. ▶ From this point the route runs much closer to the lake, rising and then dropping down again through the trees.

Around 15 min after leaving Caprino you'll pass through **Cantine di Caprino**, a tiny hamlet where there's also a *grotto*; some 10–15 min later the route takes you right across the terrace of another eating place, the **Grotto dei Pescatori** – at busy times you'll actually find yourself dodging waiters busily serving customers. ▶

Beyond the Grotto dei Pescatori the scenery becomes wilder. The well-made track rises and falls through the forest with walkers negotiating the steepest parts of the route with the help of steps and handrails. Breaks in the

Some 5–10 min along this track a sign on the path points L to the Grotto San Rocco (closed Monday), a popular waterside bar-restaurant situated couple of minutes away down flights of steps.

The Grotto dei Pescatori is a pricey fish restaurant whose well-heeled clientele reach this isolated spot by private launch from Lugano.

*The frontier marked
at Cantine di Gandria,
at the end of the walk*

trees allow for fine views across the water to Gandria (see Walk 1). After 35 min some holiday chalets announce the western edge of Cantine di Gandria, a low-key spread of *grotti* and villas that end at the tall **Museo Dogane** (Customs Museum) and its adjacent **debarcadero**, where the walk terminates.

The arm of the lake east from here is wholly in Italian territory (the inaccessible border is around 100m further on from the museum). The **Museum** (www.museodogane.ch; open Tues–Sun early April to late Oct noon–5pm; free entry) occupies a former customs house and tells the history of smuggling along the parts of Lake Lugano that straddle Switzerland and Italy.

WALK 3

San Salvatore to Morcote

Start	Top station of San Salvatore funicular railway
Finish	Morcote Piazza Grande bus stop
Distance	10km (6.25 miles)
Ascent	250m
Descent	850m
Difficulty	Grade 2
Walking time	3 hr 45 min
Terrain	The walk is mostly on well-worn forest footpaths – plus vehicle tracks and some metalled roads; virtually all of it is downhill (steeply in a small section at the start).
Refreshments	Grocery stores are thin on the ground on this walk, though there are cafes and restaurants in a couple of the villages. Stock up on snacks and water at the Migros supermarket (closed Sun) on Via Geretta in Paradiso before heading for the funicular base station around 200m away.

Every visitor to Lugano knows San Salvatore as the distinctive sugar-loaf mountain that overlooks the city from the south. With the San Salvatore funicular railway taking the strain in terms of ascent, this walk from the summit to the beautiful but rather touristy lakeside village of Morcote is inevitably mostly downhill, and for the most part takes walkers through peaceful forest whose clearings often offer frequent and enticing glimpses of the azure-blue lake and the surrounding peaks. The walk also cuts right through a verdant subtropical garden and takes in a museum, two fine churches, and a couple of typically rustic villages where *osteria* provide the opportunity for an enticing if leisurely mid-walk break.

ACCESS

The base station of the San Salvatore funicular railway is located in the Lugano suburb of Paradiso, less than 5 min on foot from Lugano-Paradiso train station (a stop for local trains heading south from Lugano), and from the Via San Salvatore bus stop, served by bus #2 (from the train station). In Morcote, buses for Lugano (and for Melide railway station, for local trains to Lugano) pull up in the Piazza Grande. Lake Lugano's tourist boats serve Paradiso, whose *debarcadero* is a 5-min walk from the base station of the funicular, and Morcote, where boats dock less than a minute's walk from the Piazza Grande.

SAN SALVATORE AND ITS FUNICULAR

The funicular was built in 1890 to allow access to the San Salvatore viewpoint; the journey is in two stages, with passengers transferring between trains at the intermediate station, Pazzallo. The second stage has an eye-wateringly steep maximum gradient of 61 per cent. At the top it's a short walk to the summit and a chapel built in the early eighteenth century by the Archfraternity of Good Death and Prayer, whose members took it upon themselves to comfort and pray for Lugano's condemned prisoners in the days and hours leading up to their execution. You can learn more about this cult in the museum (no entry charge) beside the path leading to the summit, which also includes exhibits on the area's geology and on the lightning research centre that was established here (apparently the mountain top is particularly prone to strikes); there's also some chunky electronic equipment from yesteryear associated with the transmission masts that dominate the summit.

The path begins to the S of the palatial restaurant building across from the funicular top station. The first stage drops steeply down into the forest via a number of stepped sections (which will be awkward and slippery after rain).

Monte San Salvatore is unusual in this part of the Alps – an intrusion of Dolomite limestone in an area otherwise dominated by granite. The rock was formed some 245m years ago from the bodies of tiny sea creatures that fell to the bottom of a tropical

A view from the
path as it drops
down into Morcote

The route does
not go through the
centre of Carona,
which is a larger and
more attractively
rustic village than
Ciona, with plenty
of opportunities
for eating.

sea – before being lifted up to its current height by
the tectonic contortions that formed the Alps.

After 20 min the path becomes a paved road, the Via
San Salvatore, which enters the village of **Ciona** after just
5 min; an *osteria* (closed Weds) overlooks the village's
car park (and bus stop) but there's no shop. Crossing the
main road at the car park's entrance the route plunges
back into the forest along the Via Roccolo, a wide and
easily walkable forest track that emerges onto a minor
road after 15 min; taking a left turn followed immediately by a right takes you along a narrow lane to a track
marker post by the **Grotto del Pan Perdü** on the edge of
Carona. ◄

From the track marker post opposite the *grotto* pick
up the sign to Morcote and Vico Morcote which sends
you along Via Santa Marta. After 5 min you reach a track
junction outside the **Piscina Carona**, showing directions
to Morcote via San Grato. After a 2-min walk along the
road the signs send you back into the forest along a track

that leads, after 10 min, to the **Parco San Grato**, a botanical garden full of lush subtropical plants. There's 24-hour access to the garden (www.parcosangrato.ch; no entry charge), which is famed for its azaleas, rhododendrons and conifers – though explanation boards are only in Italian and German. The entrance to the park marks the start of a steady upward climb, first through the gardens and then through more forest; there's a maze of paths but the signs will keep you on the correct route. On eventually reaching a paved road at a hairpin, bear R up the road; after 100m a sign points you into the trees and after another 80m a track marker post marks the top of the climb (15 min from the park entrance). Following the signs to Alpe Vicania and Morcote, some 25 min later another marker post situated by a patch of meadowland known as **Alpe Vicania** sends you down (L) via steps and minor roads to **Vico Morcote**, Morcote's upper town – reached in just 10 min from Alpe Vicania.

The route as it passes through Morcote

A minute's detour could take you down to the Baroque church of Santi Fedele, whose icing-sugar stucco frontage can be seen from the road as it approaches the piazza.

An irregularly shaped cobbled piazza forms the heart of Vico Morcote. ◄ From the piazza follow the directions to Morcote that take you along Strada al Castel, past Vico Morcote's *casa communale* and then L down secluded lanes and flights of steps, following the red and white stripes painted on walls and the road. In 15 min these bring you to Morcote's **Chiesa di Santa Maria del Sasso** church (with the **Oratorio San Antonio de Padova** next door, with its distinctive columned portico). From the grassy courtyard that abuts the church's southern side a long flight of steps drops down to **Morcote** itself, bringing you to the town's lakeside Piazza Grande (for the bus stop) in just 5 min.

WALK 4
Monte Caslano

Start/finish	Caslano *debarcadero*
Distance	6.5km (4 miles)
Ascent/descent	250m
Difficulty	Grade 2
Walking time	2 hr
Terrain	Forest paths with some metalled roads
Refreshments	A number of restaurants and cafes cluster around the *debarcadero*. En route, the walk passes the Hotel Fonte dei Fiori in Torrazza, which has a restaurant.

Monte Caslano is a dome-like protrusion of pale rock, fringed with cliffs and lapped by water on three sides, that rises to the southwest of Lugano, hard up against the Italian border. Its wooded slopes make for ideal easy walking territory – particularly when poor weather (or snow covering) sends walkers down to lower altitudes (the highest point on this walk is a mere 525m). There are some steep ascents and descents (which are just strenuous enough to push this walk into Grade 2) – and only one highlight, the glorious lake itself, whether viewed from the lookout point at the summit of Monte Caslano or from the paths that run high above the lake in the first part of the walk, or along its shoreline in the second. Beguiling Caslano itself has a waterside piazza with restaurant tables set out under a shady covering of trees – indeed its lake frontage is a very pleasant surprise if you walk here from the station, through a very mundane district of residential apartment blocks.

ACCESS

By tourist boat from Lugano, or take a train from Lugano's FLP station (see Public transport) to Caslano (four hourly, 26 min journey time) from where it's a 10-min level walk to the *debarcadero*.

From the **debarcadero** turn left past the Ostello Battello and follow the road as it curls R up the hill. Just 50m beyond the Ostello turn L onto the Via Stremadone which rises into the trees, becoming a track after 10 min. Just a couple of minutes later a track marker post at the top of a short flight of steps (L) points the way to Monte Caslano.

The path climbs up further through the trees, taking you first in a SE direction then SW. ▸ Some 20 min from the track marker post another marker sends you R (N) inland from the lake on another climb, at the top of which marker posts direct you R (E) to the summit of **Monte Caslano** (reached after 40 min from the debarcadero).

The path is well-made and maintained throughout, with steps in places, and gives fine views over the lake.

From the small **chapel of San Nicolao** at the summit of Monte Caslano (525m) there are predictably fine views which stretch North across Caslano towards Agno (with its airport runway) and the western fringes of Lugano.

On leaving the summit, retrace your steps for a couple of minutes and pick up the sign on the track marker post to Torrazza. After 10–15 min there's a very short path down to a lookout over the Italian town of Lavena.

The thin, river-like sliver of lake on the south side of the Caslano peninsula forms the border, with Italy almost within touching distance – though there's no crossing point here. Some 5–10 min later another track marker post points L (W) and sends you down a steep path for 15 min that brings you onto a metalled road and then into the small lakeside village of **Torrazza**.

At the T junction turn L (E) along Via Torrazza, passing the **Hotel Fonte dei Fiori** and forking R soon after to join a metalled road following the lake shore. ◄ Some 5 min beyond the factory the metalled road turns into a track beside a low-key bathing area and for 20 min after that it hugs the lake shore until once again becoming a

On the left now are the ruins of a former hydrated lime and fertilizer factory, the Fornace di Caslano, with its distinctive dome-capped kiln.

Map scale is 1:40,000

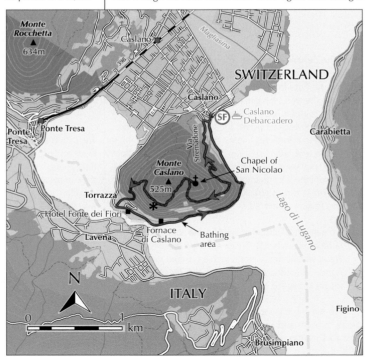

66

metalled road when **Caslano** is sighted. The **debarcadero** is reached 5 min later (a total of 40 min from the hotel in Torrazza).

Caslano, photographed from the last section of the walk

WALK 5
Monte San Giorgio

Start/finish	Top station of Brusino-Arsizio to Serpiano cable car
Distance	7.25km (4.5 miles)
Ascent/descent	500m
Difficulty	Grade 2
Walking time	2 hr 30 min
Terrain	Well-made woodland paths
Refreshments	At the restaurant beside the cable car top station; en route, at Alpe Brusino and the Hotel Serpiano.

The thickly-wooded peninsula that divides the two southerly arms of Lake Lugano makes for an area of relatively straightforward walking on an intricate network of well-maintained, well-signposted, well-marked and well-graded forest paths. It's a popular walking area and this walk, which takes you to the highest point of the peninsula – Monte San Giorgio, from where there's a predictably fabulous view over Lugano and its lake – also takes in two refreshment stops (also with views) in the form of a traditional alpine hut and a rather more luxurious hideaway resort hotel. Virtually all the walk is in trees and with the highest point being at just below 1100m this walk might be a good bet for a poor-weather morning or afternoon. The cable car from the lakeside village of Brusino-Arsizio takes care of much of the ascent, though there is a fairly steep section up through the trees at one point which just tips this walk into the '2' category.

ACCESS

The base station of the cable car is on bus route #532 from Capolago-Riva San Vitale station (hourly service; 9 min journey time), which is a stop for local trains heading south from Lugano (hourly service, 15 min journey time). Lake Lugano's tourist boats also call at a jetty a minute's walk away. There's also road access (though no bus service) to the cable car's top station, from the South. The cable car operates May–Oct Weds–Sun only.

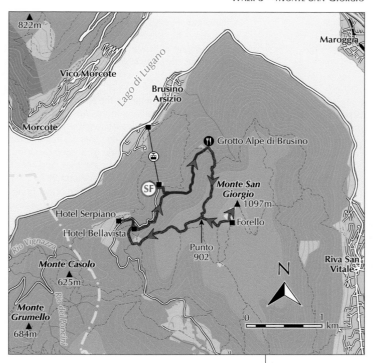

From the cable car top station pick up the route to Alpe di Brusino signed on the upper of the two track marker posts. The route snakes up through the forest on an old metalled road. Ignore the track junction after 5 min and instead, 1 min later, at a hairpin bend, head down the road past the sign for Grotto Alpe di Brusino. Some 10–15 min later you should ignore the metalled road turning off to the R; you reach **Alpe di Brusino** just a couple of minutes later (20 min from the cable car station).

> The rustic-style **grotto** serves lunch and snacks (mixed cheese platters and salami, for instance, or polenta with mushrooms) amidst a pleasant grove

in the chestnut forests. There's a basic terrace with a view through a gap in the trees towards Lugano and the summit of Monte San Salvatore (see Walk 3), which is easily identifiable thanks to its transmission tower.

The going gets more difficult now, with just under an hour of uphill walking ahead of you – steep in places.

The track marker post beside the *grotto* points you up some steps beside the building in the direction of Monte San Giorgio. ◄ After 5 min, walk straight across an intersecting track and up some zig-zags. After 10 min of these the walk undulates along the side of a steep slope but after another 10 min there are more zig-zags, and after 5 min you reach the track marker post at **Punto 902**.

Here you are signed L on a steady climb that brings you after 10–15 min to a junction (for a L turn) and then after 5 min to a deserted building at **Forello**. Turn L here for the final climb to the (also deserted) building at the summit of **Monte San Giorgio** (reached after 5–10 min).

The summit of **Monte San Giorgio** (1097m) provides a wonderfully panoramic view over Lugano, its lake and its mountain hinterland. It's a UNESCO world heritage site on account of the middle Triassic period fossils found here. The fossils are around 225 million years old and are of land-based as well as sea-based creatures (this part of the Alps was once sea floor before it was folded into the mountains seen today). There's a museum of fossils at Meride, 3km to the south of the walking area (closed Mon).

Some 20 min from Punto 902 there's an information board (in English) about the geology and fossils of the local area.

From the summit of Monte San Giorgio it's necessary to retrace your steps to **Punto 902** (reached after 20 min) where you are signed L to Serpiano. Follow the path as it runs through the forest and then becomes a deep cutting in the hillside. ◄ Just a couple of minutes beyond the information board you are signed R through a clearing in the trees. A minute later another track marker post sends you R (to Serpiano) along an easy, level track. After just a couple more minutes a

succession of marker posts point you L then R, sending you onto a track that soon curls above a parking area and drops you after 10 min onto a road beside the boarded-up **Hotel Bellavista**. The modern grey façade of the **Hotel Serpiano** is visible just to the W.

The view towards Lugano enjoyed by walkers from the summit of Monte San Giorgio

The **Hotel Serpiano** is a modern three-star spa hotel (www.serpiano.ch/en) with a fantastic terrace – it's well worth stopping just for a coffee and a rest up to enjoy the panoramic view, though facilities also include an indoor heated swimming pool, a sauna and a steam bath if you want to make an afternoon of it! There's a bus service from outside the front of the hotel to Mendrisio station (for trains to Lugano) but there are only two services a day.

Morcote, viewed from the Hotel Serpiano, one of the refreshment places the walk passes

From the hotel head back to the track marker post by the **Hotel Bellavista**, which points you back into the forest to the cable car station. Head up the steps and take a L turn for the well-made track that runs above the road. After 20 min turn L at a marker post for a track that will drop you at the cable car top station after just a couple of minutes.

WALK 6

Monte Tamaro to Monte Lema

Start	Top station of the Monte Tamaro cable car (Alpe Foppa)
Finish	Top station of the Monte Lema cable car
Distance	12.5km (7.75 miles)
Ascent	850m
Descent	820m
Difficulty	Grade 3
Walking time	5 hr 30 min
Terrain	Vehicle track to begin with, then steep, rocky mountain paths (with some scrambling)
Refreshments	In its early stages the walk passes by a mountain hut with a café. Beyond this, enterprising local farmers set up self-service stalls selling drinks at regular intervals (payment is by honesty box) – though these can't be relied on out-of-season. Between Rivera-Bironico station and the cable car base station you'll pass a handy Denner supermarket, though it's closed on Sundays.

This is counted as one of the classic Ticino walks – if not *the* classic. Running along the top of the spine of the hills that separate Lake Lugano from Lake Maggiore, the walk affords spectacular views over both lakes – and as the walk takes you to an altitude of nearly 2000m there are fine views too towards the heart of the Alps. Though tough going, with a series of steep ascents and descents, the walk is very popular – and you haven't really 'walked' Ticino until it's under your belt. Be warned, though, that the walk takes in exposed ridges and summits and will be treacherous during storms and high winds (when the cable cars close); this is one walk that it really pays to leave until a fine day, though the sun can be wearying and shade is in very short supply along the route.

ACCESS

The base station of the Monte Tamaro cable car is at Rivera, a 5-min walk from Rivera-Bironico railway station (walk R along the main road and it's behind the dome of the aquapark); the base station of the Monte Lema cable car is at Miglieglia, linked by bus to Lamone-Cadempino railway station (hourly or every 2 hours; 55 min) for a train back to Rivera-Bironico (twice hourly; 11 min). Both stations are served by local trains running between Lugano and Bellinzona. This walk is so popular that in summer dedicated minibuses are laid on at the end of the afternoon to take walkers directly from the cable car base station at Miglieglia to the base station of the Monte Tamaro cable car at Rivera: the tickets can only be bought at the Monte Tamaro cable car base station. The price for a ticket that takes you up on the first cable car, down on the second and then back by bus to the Monte Tamaro cable car base station is 55 Francs for adults and 30 Francs for children aged 6–15.

The chapel beside the cable car station at the start of the walk

ALPE FOPPA

Alpe Foppa, at the top of the Monte Tamaro cable car, is something of a tourist playground, with a huge restaurant, a kids' play area, and a luge (dry bobsleigh) run. Something not to miss, however, is the starkly modernist Santa Maria degli Angeli chapel, designed by the Ticino architect Mario Botta (b.1943) and built between 1992 and 1996. The exterior consists of a series of walkways, passageways and viewing platforms that overlook an extraordinary panorama, while the interior of the chapel features paintings by the Italian artist Enzo Cucchi (b.1949).

The track marker post by the top station of the cable car at **Alpe Foppa** sends you SW along a vehicle track that twists slowly up to the transmission mast and associated buildings that can be clearly seen from the cable car station (reckon on around 50 min to reach them). Head past the transmission station for 5 min to reach **Capanna Tamaro**, perched on a ledge. ▶ The route actually takes you right across the outdoor terrace of the *capanna* and then on along a path towards Monte Tamaro, the ascent of which takes 25 min from the *capanna*.

The capanna (www.utoe. ch/?page_id=30; Tel. 091 946 10 08) is the only reliable place serving refreshments along the whole length of the walk; it can also provide accommodation.

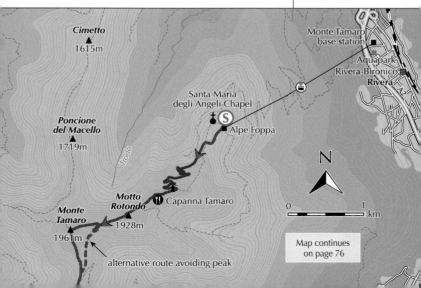

A clearly-marked turning L just before the final ascent of **Monte Tamaro** allows for a shortcut that avoids climbing up to the mountain's summit; it rejoins the described route on the South side of the peak.

Enjoying the view at Capanna Tamaro

The final ascent of **Monte Tamaro** is a rocky scramble in places but it's worth it – from the top you can look down in one direction over Lake Maggiore, with Locarno clearly visible, while a sliver of Lake Lugano is also visible in the far distance. At 1961m the summit is 430m higher than the cable car top station and is the highest point on the walk.

The path down from Monte Tamaro is also hard-going but eventually levels off onto a ridge. Some 45 min from the summit there's a hut where at busy times you can help yourself to drinks and snacks, dropping some coins into an honesty box. ▸ The ascent of **Monte Gradiccioli** starts immediately beyond the hut, from where you should reckon on 25 min to reach the top (1936m).

Leaving the summit of Monte Gradiccioli it's a steady drop down (45 min) to the stone hut at **Passo d'Agario**;

Immediately beyond the hut a turning R allows for a short cut that avoids the ascent of Monte Gradiccioli; it rejoins the described route S of the summit.

The Swiss–Italian border is a few metres W of the ridge at this point; the villages that you can see amidst the forest to the R are all in Italy.

shelter and more honesty-box refreshments (the last on the walk) should be available here. You're now on the last section of the walk, with Monte Lema around 1 hr 30 min away. Beyond the hut at Agario the route shelters in the lee of the summit of **Monte Magno** (which it doesn't ascend) before rising once again onto the exposed ridge. A basic hut allows for shelter at **Zottone**, and beyond this the path becomes trickier, with railings and hand-held cables to assist walkers as the track rises and falls along the undulating ridge. ◀

As you make progress along the ridge the views over Lugano and its lake become more enticing – and the cluster of buildings on the summit of Monte Lema get steadily closer. But they're further away than you think, because around an hour after leaving Passo d'Agario the path begins to drop right down to a low saddle, leaving walkers with a final steep ascent to the summit of Monte Lema: take the track up and then the steps on the L. **Monte Lema** is much less busy than Monte Tamaro: a bar-restaurant with a spectacular outdoor terrace is the only building keeping the cable car top station company.

WALK 7
Monte Boglia and the Denti della Vecchia

Start	Brè Paese bus stop
Finish	Cimadera Paese bus stop
Distance	14km (8.75 miles)
Ascent	1150m
Descent	860m
Difficulty	Grade 3
Walking time	5 hr 30 min
Terrain	Mostly well-made woodland paths, though with some challengingly steep sections; metalled roads and vehicle tracks at the start and end.
Refreshments	En route, at the Alpe Bolla and Alpe Pairolo mountain huts; no shops or cafes at beginning or end.

This fabulous long-distance walk, which starts at the end of one of Lugano's city bus routes and ends in a village in its mountainous hinterland, provides two highlights – an ascent of Monte Boglia, whose summit offers one of the most jaw-dropping panoramas in Ticino, and a chance to walk through the Denti della Vecchia, an area of spectacularly toothy limestone pinnacles that rise from deep beech forests and provide habitats for ravens, falcons and kestrels. Two mountain huts keep you refreshed along the way and although there are some challengingly steep sections on the way up to Monte Boglia, the rewards in terms of scenery make this walk thoroughly worthwhile. However, you need to choose a fine day – both to appreciate the views and because the ascent of Monte Boglia takes you over some exposed ridges.

ACCESS

Brè Paese is the last stop for local bus #B12 from Lugano Centro (twice hourly, journey time 27 min); from Cimadera, buses are every 60–90 min to Sonvico or Tesserete, where you must change for a bus to Lugano Centro; total journey time 50–60 min.

The walk begins in the car park at **Brè** where Paese bus stop is situated.

> **Brè** is an attractive stone-built village nestling on the NE flanks of cone-shaped Monte Brè, which overlooks Lugano from the E. An alternative start to this walk would be to take the funicular from Lugano up to Monte Brè and then take the stepped path down (the Scalinata alla Torretta) from the summit to Brè itself (1 km).

The first track marker post directs you to Alpe Bolla along a cobbled lane, the Via Lavatoio. After just a minute walking through the village another track marker post directs you R along the Sentiero Alpe Bolla which takes you NE, crossing the Via Pineta three times. The fourth time you cross this metalled road, some 15 min after leaving the car park, you leave the village behind and

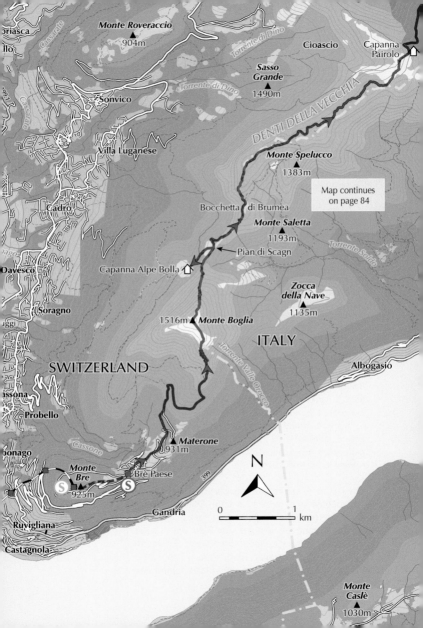

Monte Roveraccio
904m

Cassarat

Cioascio

Capanna
Pairolo

riasca

llo

Torrente di Dino

Sasso
Grande
1490m

Sonvico

Torrente di Dino

DENTI DELLA VECCHIA

Villa Luganese

Monte Spelucco
1383m

Map continues
on page 84

Cadro

Bocchetta di Brumea

Monte Saletta
1193m

Torrente Solda

Pian di Scagn

Davesco

Capanna Alpe Bolla

Soragno

Zocca
della Nave
1135m

ggi

1516m Monte Boglia

ITALY

SWITZERLAND

Torrente Valle Oracco

Albogasio

ssona

Probello

Cassone

Materone
931m

bonago

399

Monte
Bre

Brè Paese

S   S

N

925m

Gandria

Ruvigliana

0   1

km

Castagnola

Monte
Caslè
1030m

follow the cobbled Sentiero Alpe Bolla as it climbs up into the forest.

5–10 min later a track marker post offers two ways to Monte Boglia. Take the shorter of the two ways (around the hairpin) and after 10 min turn R at the next track marker post and then, after another 10 min, L at another track marker post. It's a steep ascent up through the forest for the next 30 min until another track marker post points R and the gradient lessens off. ▶ Gradually the path climbs out of the treeline giving views towards the bald, grassy summit of **Monte Boglia**, which is reached some 35 min after the track marker post at the top of the main ascent.

> **Monte Boglia** (1516m), surmounted by a cross, sits on the Swiss–Italian border and offers a truly awe-inspiring panoramic view that takes in Lugano and the curling arms of its lake; Lake Maggiore as far as the Italian resort of Stresa; and to the East, Lake

Monte Boglia (top left of frame), the distinctive peak overlooking Lugano from the east, is ascended at the start of this walk

5–10 min later there's a fantastic view R towards the Italian resort of Porlezza, at Lake Lugano's eastern end, with a sliver of Lake Como visible beyond.

Como, the most famous of Northern Italy's lakes, in its deep valley. To the south, beyond Monte Generoso and Monte San Giorgio, the landscape flattens out onto the North Italian Plain, while to the North, in the far distance, the view stretches towards the high ridges of the Swiss Alps. The various individual peaks can be identified using a panorama, while benches allow you to take in the views at leisure.

Alpe Bolla is signed from the summit of Monte Boglia. The path down into and then through the forest is well-made, with steps in places, and follows the line of the international border, although there are no markers to indicate this. The trees gradually give way to pastureland and 35 min from the summit of Monte Boglia a marker post in a field at **Pian di Scagn** points L to **Alpe Bolla**, reached after a walk of 5 min through the trees.

The **Capanna Alpe Bolla** (1129m) is one of a group of buildings in a sunny location overlooking the villages that make up the straggling northern extension of Lugano. Basic meals are served and there is accommodation available (091 943 2570). If you wish to shorten this walk there are paths from here down to Cureggia, Cadro and Sonvico (all 1–2 hours) for buses to Lugano.

To continue the walk, retrace your steps to **Pian di Scagn** and take the path NE marked for Cimadera and Capanna Pairolo. ◀ There are some steep uphill sections now. After 30 min you pass the **Bocchetta di Brumea** track marker post and 10 min later is the sign that announces the start of the **Denti della Vecchia** forest reserve, with the most impressive sheer vertical rock face (to the L of the path) encountered some 25 min after that.

Once again the path here follows the line of the unmarked international frontier.

The **Denti della Vecchia** (literally, 'teeth of the old woman') are a series of gnarled grey dolomite limestone pinnacles (clearly visible from Lugano) whose profile look like a series of rotten teeth, hence the

The view from the Denti della Vecchia

name. The path runs along what may be considered the 'gum', just below the exposed 'teeth', with the rock faces rising on the L and then the R. The surrounding forests are beech and pine. The area has long been a favourite of climbers and you might see some dare-devil figures high above you on some of the sheer cliff faces.

Beyond the main rock face the path passes a track marker post (after 5 min) and then skirts below some vertical cliff faces with occasional ropes and chains attached to the cliff to aid walkers. Some 25 min beyond the track marker post, ignore the turn R to Cresita and Sasso Palazzo (both in Italy) and instead fork left and down the hill. ▶ The path now undulates through the forest, emerging into pastureland after 20 min; the **Capanna Pairolo** is reached 15 min later (35 min in total from the junction where you fork L).

At this point the path finally leaves the ridge that forms the border and you can count yourself as being properly in Switzerland.

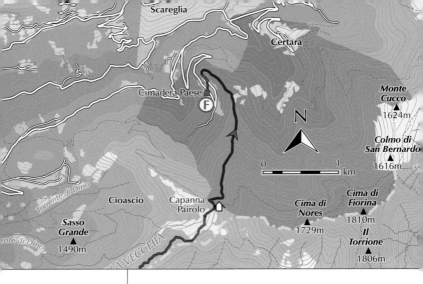

The **Capanna Pairolo** (www.capanna-pairolo.ch/en; 091 944 1156) offers drinks and simple meals to walkers and can also provide accommodation. It's a popular base for climbers and mountain bikers and has been operational since 1937. On clear days the view from its terrace can stretch as far as the Monte Rosa and Mischabel massifs, which include some of the highest peaks in the Alps.

From the *capanna* take the vehicle track that rises behind the hut to the top of the ridge and then take the vehicle track that leads down from the other side of the ridge into the trees. After 25 min you're signed L into the upper parts of the village of **Cimadera** and the track becomes a metalled road. You won't see the main part of the village until the last moment as it's behind a steep bluff which the road rounds in a hairpin (45 min from the *capanna*). Some 120m on from the hairpin look for the flight of steps that take you down R along pedestrianized lanes through the centre of the village and to the car park and bus stop.

WALK 8

Monte Bar and the Capriasca Valley

Start	Cortiasca Paese Bus Stop
Finish	Roveredo Paese Bus Stop
Distance	13.25km (8.25 miles)
Ascent	900m
Descent	1200m
Difficulty	Grade 3
Walking time	5 hr
Terrain	Well-made and well-graded forest and mountain paths
Refreshments	The Eco Hotel Locanda del Giglio at Roveredo (200m from the bus stop and signed from the path) has a restaurant. There's no shop here, or at Cortiasca. The Capanna Monte Bar and Capanna La Ginestra can supply refreshments en route.

The highlight of this walk is unquestionably the jaw-dropping panorama from the summit of Monte Bar, the rounded, grass-topped mountain that overlooks Lugano from the north and which provides views that reach deep into Northern Italy and towards the high Alps of Central Switzerland. Views over Lugano from the viewpoint at Motto della Croce are also wonderful. This lengthy walk also takes in two *capannas*, the stylish Capanna Monte Bar situated on an open hillside just below the summit of that mountain, and the more traditional Capanna La Ginestra, at a lower altitude and surrounded by the woodland of the picturesque Capriasca valley. While the walk rises to an altitude of 1816m the paths are not as challenging as they sometimes are at this altitude – although with the views comes a fairly strenuous initial ascent. Time your walk carefully to take account of the sparsity of the bus service back from Roveredo, and choose a fine day – not only would it be a shame to end up with the views obscured by clouds, but much of the first part of the walk is above the treeline, and highly exposed.

ACCESS

Both bus stops are on the #B448 bus route from Tesserete Stazione to Maglio di Colla (every 2 hours); journey times 18 min (to Cortiasca) and 8 min (from Roveredo). Bus #B461 runs twice hourly from Lugano Centro and Lugano Station to Tesserete Stazione (journey time 22 min). There is no train station at Tesserete (despite the name of the bus stop).

The track marker posts by the bus stop at **Cortiasca** offer four different routes to Monte Bar, each with a different timing – so it pays to make sure you are on the right one. The route presented here rises up through the settlement,

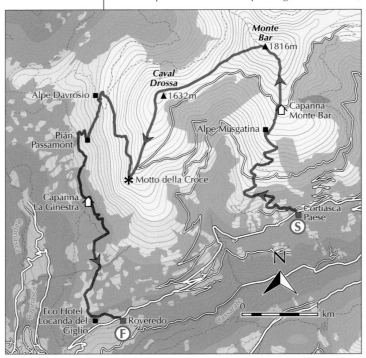

The Capanna Monte Bar, overlooking Lugano from just below the summit of Monte Bar

via the steps by the bus stop, to the road that runs parallel with the main road at a higher altitude. Turn L (W) here along a road lined with pastel-coloured houses and follow it as it curls around over a river, the Riale d'Albumo. You are then directed R across a patch of grass and immediately L, the path curling around behind some farm buildings and crossing another stream. ▶ The path now snakes up the hillside into meadowland.

Some 30 min after leaving the bus stop you reach a track marker post amidst pastureland that signposts Capanna Monte Bar, and 15 min later is another marker post beside some picnic tables which sends you up to a metalled road; this road is crossed and then actually joined shortly afterwards. Follow the road as far as the private and splendidly isolated private dwelling at **Alpe Musgatina**, reached an hour from the bus stop. From here take the path that rises behind the dwelling across exposed cattle pastures; 10 min beyond the house you will see the **Capanna Monte Bar** on the hillside – it's another 10 min of fairly stiff ascent to reach it after that.

The **Capanna Monte Bar** (https://capannamontebar. casticino.ch; 091 966 3322) was opened in 2016 and is a thoroughly contemporary and stylish

There are good views on this section of the route over towards the limestone pinnacles known as the Denti della Vecchia (see Walk 7) on the other side of the valley.

structure faced largely in dark wood. Its setting on an exposed slope apparently in the middle of absolutely nowhere is probably its most compelling aspect, though the expansive terrace and the bright and airy refectory come a close second. There's sleeping accommodation for 60 people and a fabulous sunrise to wake up to for those who spend the night here.

From the *capanna* it's a fairly steep 30-min climb to the summit of **Monte Bar** (1816m), using the path that leads N from behind the hut and crosses the bald grassy expanse of the hill. The view from the summit is magnificent, encompassing Lakes Lugano and Maggiore and stretching deep into Italy. From the summit take the path that runs W, dropping down then rising to the (lower) neighbouring peak, **Caval Drossa** (1632m), reached after 15 min. From here a path runs S over the exposed hillside for 50 min down to the viewpoint over Lugano from the enormous cross set in a stone plinth at **Motto della Croce** (not to be confused with the viewpoint over Bellinzona with the same name – see Walk 22).

This is a picturesque valley, scattered with farms and tiny settlements.

From Motto della Croce take the path that runs N along the E side of the Capriasca valley. ◄ The well-made path drops down steadily to the farm buildings at **Alpe Davrosio** (25 min) where you should take the track down to another farm building. Here you are signed S along a path that again runs along the flank of the valley, this time at a much lower altitude, before dropping down into trees at **Pián Passamónt**. The path continues S through the cluster of buildings at Sorè, 10 min beyond which a sign points L up through the trees to **Capanna La Ginestra**, reached after another 10 min (a total of 1hr 15 min from Motto della Croce).

The convivial **Capanna La Ginestra** (950m) has an idyllic setting among birch and chestnut woods and gets its name from the bushes of flowering gorse that characterize the valley. There is sleeping accommodation and refreshments are offered, but

the *capanna* may not be open every day, even in summer – check online in advance if a stop here is an important part of your itinerary.

The track marker post by the southern gate to the *capanna* now points L to Roveredo. The path drops steadily down through the trees, with woodland gradually giving way to farm buildings and villas before paved, stepped lanes take you down through the centre of **Roveredo** to the bus stop on the road (40 min from the *capanna*).

The viewpoint Motto della Croce, overlooking Lugano

WALK 9
Cima di Medeglia and the old Military Road

Start	Isone Gròssa Bus Stop
Finish	Rivera-Bironico Railway Station
Distance	11.5km (7 miles)
Ascent	570m
Descent	850m
Difficulty	Grade 2
Walking time	4 hr
Terrain	Vehicle tracks and well-made forest paths
Refreshments	There are two restaurants in Isone but no shop. There are cafés and a Denner supermarket across the road from Rivera-Bironico station.

The highlight of this walk is undoubtedly the view from Cima di Medeglia, the high ridge that separates Lugano and the Southern Ticino from Bellinzona and Lake Maggiore to the North. There's an initial ascent right at the start of the walk, up from Isone, but the walk's central section is along an old military road running above the valley of the Ticino River, meaning that gradients are comparatively gentle. Indeed, this is the easiest and lowest of the four walks that explore the region north and northeast of Lugano (it rarely strays above the tree line). It's also the most accessible with regards to public transport access – and on top of this the walk gives an excellent insight into the region's history and geography: the ridge the walk traverses is an important cultural dividing line in Ticino, while the military road points to the history of the area as for centuries being vulnerable to invasion from the south.

ACCESS

Bus #B454 runs every two hours from outside Rivera-Bironico station (served by half-hourly local trains from Lugano; journey time 15 min) to Isone Gròssa (journey time 16 min).

The first track marker post is just a few steps up the road from the bus stop and sends you up the hill (L) on a metalled lane, A Grossa, towards Cima di Dentro. After 5 min turn R at the hairpin onto a forest path that runs NE along an old valley-side mule track before there's a reasonably steep ascent that rises onto a metalled road (30 min from the hairpin). Follow the road N for under 5 min as it drops down to **Cima di Dentro**, then turn L (sign posted Riviera Stazione on the marker post) onto a vehicle track. This is the old military road (*strada militare*), which runs W.

THE OLD MILITARY ROAD

Since the Swiss Confederation took control of Ticino at the very end of the Middle Ages, the area has been heavily defended against attack from the south. The initial defensive line was at Bellinzona, but when the rail line to the Gotthard Pass was built in the nineteenth century, attention moved further south to Monte Ceneri, the ridge that divides Lugano and Southern Ticino from Bellinzona and the approach to the Gotthard. (The rail line to the Gotthard burrowed under the ridge in a tunnel – and nowadays there are two further tunnels, for the motorway and for high-speed trains.) The rail line was considered such a strategic asset that at the start of the twentieth century it was considered necessary to fortify Monte Ceneri and the ridge extending southeast from there to the high point of Cima di Medeglia. Work began on constructing barracks, ammunition stores and gun emplacements in 1913 and continued through the First World War. Part of the work involved the construction of a military access road from Robasacco in the Ticino valley up to Cima di Medeglia, which was completed in 1914 and was built by a mixture of military and civilian workers (the route described on this walk follows the track as it runs along the northern flank of the ridge, overlooking the Ticino valley). The area has been a site of military activity ever since, most notably since 1973 in the form of the Grenadier School at Isone, where elite special forces of the Swiss Army are trained. Not surprisingly the training areas and associated barracks are off-limits, and though walkers will see a fair bit of military signage and barriers around Cima di Dentro, army activity seems to co-exist peaceably with walkers.

The track initially skirts some farm buildings (L) – ignore the metalled road that rises L here, and further on the sign pointing R to the Capanna Neveggio (which

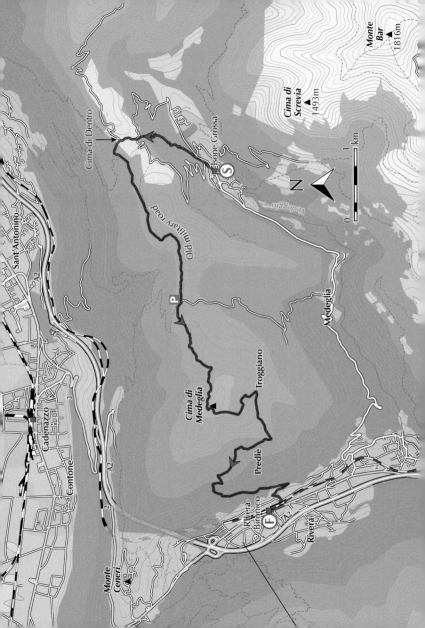

The view over Bellinzona from the Old Military Road

provides group accommodation but is not open to casual visitors). ▶ After an hour, the track passes (L) a small car park (there's road access up here from the village of Medeglia) before 20 min later you are directed off the track and R into the trees for the path up to the summit of **Cima di Medeglia**, reached after another 15 min (with a short-but-steep final section).

There's an absorbing view from the summit of **Cima di Medeglia** (1260m) encompassing Lake Maggiore, Lake Lugano, and the transmitter on the summit of Monte Tamaro (see Walk 6). The ridge is an important topographical and cultural divide in the Canton: the area to the north is the Sopraceneri ('Above Ceneri'), characterized by high mountains and isolated valleys, while that to the south is Sottoceneri ('Below Ceneri'), which is rather more urbanized and industrialized. Traditionally the inhabitants of the Sottoceneri have rather looked down on their northern counterparts as 'yokels' who lack the worldly-wise sophistication of the town-dwellers of the south.

As the trees part there are views from the track towards Bellinzona and Locarno and over the tangle of roads and rail lines approaching the Monte Ceneri tunnels.

The summit of Cima di Medeglia, which provides the scenic highlight of this walk

From the summit head along the path that runs S (keeping the transmitter ahead of you). 10–15 min later a track marker post points you L past some farm buildings to join a vehicle track. After 5–10 min there's a R turn that brings you 10 min later to the cluster of buildings at **Troggiano** where you should pick up the route to Rivera Stazione, signposted via Predlè.

It's steep descent now into the Leguana valley until the path levels off after around 20 min onto a mule track that takes you N. There's another (smaller) cluster of buildings to walk through at **Predlè** followed by two minor torrents to ford until a track marker post (15 min from Predlè) shows two ways down to Rivera. ◄

There are occasional views from these paths towards Lake Lugano – though the Leguana valley itself, busy with roads, railways, settlement and light industry, is unfortunately not the region's prettiest.

Taking the shorter route takes you S along the thickly-forested valley flanks until 45 min later you take a farm track for a R turn that takes you down into the centre of **Rivera**. There's then a L turn for the pedestrian underpass that takes you under the rail lines for the station (R along the road).

WALKS FROM LOCARNO

This bridge in Bignasco is crossed towards the end of Walk 15

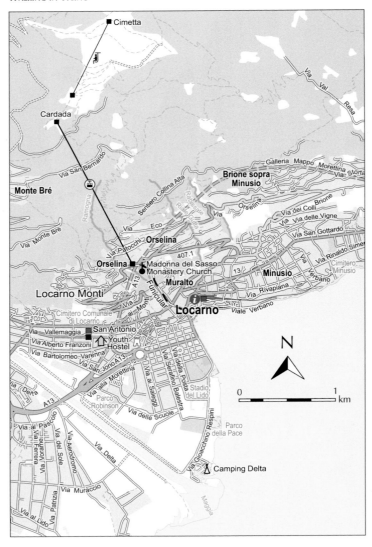

The remarkable church at Mogno is one of the highlights of Walk 15

WALKS FROM LOCARNO

As far as walkers are concerned, Locarno is all about its mountain hinterland, rather than the town itself or the spectacular lake – Lago Maggiore – on which it sits. The town is surrounded by a forest of high peaks and precipitous slopes that drop right down to the shores of the lake: the lofty viewpoint of Cimetta (1670m), with its jaw-dropping lake-and-mountain views, can be easily reached from the very centre of town – a combination of funicular railway, cable car and chairlift take care of a rise in altitude of nearly a mile. It's a good place for first-time visitors to Locarno to get their bearings – and it's the starting point for one of the walks in this section, too (Walk 12).

After that it's time to head 'inland' – away from the lake – for the walks. Although one suggested route actually runs along Locarno's lake shore (Walk 10), and another threads its way through the woods and residential districts on the hillside above the town (Walk 11), most walks in this chapter begin in one of the three valleys that converge at Locarno – collectively known as the 'Locarno Valleys' – and require a journey by bus or train from Locarno to reach their start point. These valleys offer an immense variety of walks, from routes along valley bottoms that hug the banks of fast-flowing rivers to walks that wind their way through the remote and often forbidding scenery that characterizes the geographical heart of the canton.

EXPLORING LOCARNO

Sitting on the northern tip of Lago Maggiore, the natural beauty of Locarno's setting is tough to beat. It's a much smaller city than Lugano, with none of the latter's sprawling suburbs – and with Milan that little bit further away, you'll find less of the sunglass-toting day-tripping glitterati here, too. Yet Italy seems much tangibly closer: Lake Maggiore is substantially an Italian lake, and the border is less than 10km from the outskirts of the city. That, combined with the mild weather, the palm trees, the pizzerias and the sunbathers tanning themselves by the lake, means that visitors to Locarno can find it hard to convince themselves that they are actually in Switzerland; and apart from during the annual Locarno International Film Festival in August, which fills the city up with visitors, the resort is largely a place of waterside lounging, relaxation and strolling.

In terms of what there is to see in Locarno itself, the city's major rainy-day attractions are the sanctuary-church of Madonna del Sasso,

spectacularly perched on a steep cliff above the city and very close to the start and end point of Walk 11; and the historic castle, which lies west of the city centre and was the venue for the signing of the 1922 Locarno Pact, one of the most important international treaties signed during the interwar era. And don't neglect arty Ascona, which occupies the west side of the peninsula on which Locarno spreads: just 15 min away by regular bus, it offers craft shops, art galleries, and exceptionally pretty views from the cafés and restaurants that line its handsome lakeside piazza.

ACCOMMODATION IN LOCARNO

Although there's accommodation to be found in village hotels and B&Bs along all three of Locarno's valleys (see next section), many walkers will want to base themselves in Locarno itself, which offers the most flexibility in terms accessing as many walks as possible.

There's a good variety of accommodation on offer, with the most affordable being the town's youth hostel on Via Varenna 18 (091 756 1500, https://www.youthhostel.ch/en/hostels/locarno), which is busy with walkers for much of the year: the rustle of waterproof trousers, the sighs as people lift heavy packs onto their backs and click of walking poles on shiny floors is always a familiar sound after breakfast and in the late afternoon. It's a modern, functional building set in a fairly nondescript part of town (take a local bus to Cinque Vie from the station, or it's a walk of around 15 min through the Old Town); there's wi-fi throughout and evening meals too (unless it's a quiet time of year) – and all guests receive a free Ticino Card (see the Local transport and driving section in the Introduction). Conveniently, San Antonio station on the Centovalli rail line and San Antonio bus stop on the route into the Valle Maggia are a 3-minute walk away, so you don't need to go into the centre of town to catch a bus or train to reach walking start points in either of these valleys.

There are no other hostels in Locarno. There is, however, a camp-site (https://www.campingdelta.com/en), attractively positioned by the lake 1.4km south of the station and open all year (you can rent cabins as well as pitch a tent, and it has its own private beach).

Aside from this, both Locarno and Ascona are crammed with hotels and *alloggio* – as a glance at any accommodation website will show. You'll pay a premium to stay by the lake and beware that everywhere is expensive (and books out quickly) in the summer, particularly during the film festival. Opulence is of course available for people who can afford it: for super-luxury hotels, prices tend to start at around 500 Francs per night for a standard double room in August, and head towards the stratosphere from there.

WALKING AND STAYING IN THE LOCARNO VALLEYS

The westernmost of the three 'Locarno Valleys' is the Centovalli, a narrow, twisting defile whose slopes are thick with chestnut forests. It begins at Intragna, west of Locarno, and unlike the other two valleys this one is a 'through' route, with the road and Centovalli railway both crossing the border into Italy at Camedo and continuing over a low pass to the Italian town of Domodossola. Our walk in this valley (Walk 13) runs along its northern slopes from Camedo to Intragna – though many other routes are possible, perhaps making use of the cable car that spans the valley and takes people to the village of Rasa, which has no road access. Accommodation in this valley is limited: the most obvious option is the Osteria Grütli in Camedo (osteriagrutli.ch), which the recommended walk passes right by.

East of the Centovalli is the lengthiest of the three Locarno Valleys, the Valle Maggia, characterized by broad meadows, towering waterfalls, colourful villages and roadside *grotti* (restaurants). At Bignasco, some 50 min by bus from Locarno, the valley splits, with a branch running NW to the Robiei cable car base station at San Carlo, and a second branch running NE to Fusio. Here the crowds begin to thin out, the scenery becomes more vertical and the buildings all seem to be made of grey stone.

The upper station of the Robiei cable car is the starting point for one of our high-altitude walks (Walk 16), while the Val Lavizzara between Fusio and Bignasco provides the setting for a lengthy riverside stroll (15). At Cevio, just before Bignasco, there's access to a side valley and the ski resort of Bosco Gurin, a traditionally German-speaking village that's the highest in Ticino – the starting point for another challenging high-level walk (Walk 17).

Regarding accommodation in the Valle Maggia, Bignasco is home to five guesthouses, perfect for those who want to explore this area in depth; they include the Albergo Posta (Tel 091 760 7000), with an attractive dining terrace overlooking the splashing river, and the Locanda Turisti (Tel 091 760 7020, locanda-turisti.ch/) nearby – both are very central and handy for the busy bus interchange stop at Bignasco Posta. A similar number of options can be found in Cevio, though

The Froda Waterfall can be reached on a fifteen minute walk from Sonogno

it's marginally less appealing as a place to stay – and there are hotels too in Fusio (including the modern, basic and friendly Hotel Fusio, Tel 091 600 09 00) and Bosco Gurin, though be prepared to be somewhat 'out on a limb' if you decide to stay in either of these places: it's mainly car drivers who would choose to stay somewhere this remote.

To the east of the Valle Maggia is the Val Verzasca, which opens out into Lago Maggiore at Tenero, one stop by train from Locarno. At the valley's entrance is the enormous Verzasca (or Contra) Dam, famous for its bungee jumps and its appearance in a number of movies (including the James Bond film *Goldeneye*). It's the finishing point for Walk 20, a valley walk that runs beside the churning Verzasca river. The valley beyond the dam and its reservoir is narrow and forested, and historically resonant too, with Walk 19 allowing a glimpse at former water supply systems that can still be seen amidst the high pastures. At the head of the valley (where buses from Locarno and Tenero terminate) is carless Sonogno, with a museum that looks at the history of the valley (and its long legacy of rural poverty) and a 15-minute walk to the spectacularly high Froda waterfall (take Strada de Redòrta from the Ristorante Alpino in the village centre, cross the river on the pedestrian bridge beside the sports centre and turn right for a level walk through the woods, along a trail often lined with art installations). As you might expect, dozens of walks

that penetrate deep into high and wild countryside fan out from Sonogno.

Accommodation is limited in the valley, though the Ristorante Alpino in Sonogno has affordable rooms (Tel 091 746 1163) as does the modern Campagna hotel, further down the valley at Frasco (Tel 091 746 1146).

INFORMATION AND MAPS

Locarno's tourist office – whose staff are knowledgeable about walks, and which has a good range of maps for sale – is located in the station (open 9am–6pm Mon–Fri, 10am–6pm Sat and 10am–1.30pm and 2.30-5pm Sun; no lunchtime closure July and August). It's the best place to obtain maps, and even offers a free map – Vallemaggia Wanderkarte – that shows walking routes in the Valle Maggia and the Centovalli, albeit at rather a small scale.

Also useful, at least for planning, are maps in the Travellers Maps series, which include Vallemaggia and Tenero & Valle Verzasca, and which are also free. In addition the office provides a free maps-and-information leaflet detailing the Sentiero Alta and Sentiero Bassa walks (Walk 11).

That said, it's maps in the 1:50,000 scale Schweizer Wanderwege map series produced by Swisstopo that are going to be most useful for walkers in this region, particularly 276T which covers the Centovalli, the Valle Maggia as far as Bignasco, and the Val Verzasca; unfortunately you'll need to

The village of Bosco Gurin, whose cable car is used to access the start of Walk 17

use other maps to walk outside this area – 275T for the Bosco Gurin area, 265T for the walks around Robiei and 266T for Fusio and the Val Lavizzara.

PUBLIC TRANSPORT

Trains

Locarno's train station, located a block away from the lake to the east of the old town, is the focal point for public transport users. There are frequent services to Airolo, Bellinzona, Biasca and Lugano, and services further afield too, to Zurich, Basel and Milan. Narrow gauge trains on the Centovalli line to Domodossola in Italy (see Local transport and driving) – which are needed to access Walk 13 – leave from an underground platform beneath the main station. At Domodossola they connect with mainline trains that run southeast to Milan and northwest through the Simplon tunnel to Brig (in Canton Valais), Bern and Geneva.

Bus services

Postbuses leave from the area outside the station. The most important are the #315 to Cavergno (for the Valle Maggia) and the #321 to Sonogno (for the Val Verzasca) – both packed with walkers on fine days in summer. In the Valle Maggia there are a number of separate services that connect the numerous side valleys with the main valley. Locarno is also big enough to have its own local bus network, which can be used to access the first two walks in this section.

WALK 10

Along the shore of Lake Maggiore

Start	Delta Maggia Bus Stop
Finish	Tenero train station
Distance	6km (3.75 miles)
Ascent	Negligible
Descent	Negligible
Difficulty	Grade 1
Walking time	1 hr 20 min
Terrain	Paved paths throughout
Refreshments	There are multiple cafes and shops around Locarno station (just off the route); the route passes a number of restaurants and bars in its central section and there's a café at Tenero station.

This highly accessible walk, which sticks to the lake shore almost in its entirety (and is level all the way), provides for an excellent introduction to Locarno and its seductive lake. Running through a sculpture park and past a flower garden and a sixteenth-century waterside church, the route links the southern part of Locarno with its low-key easterly extension, Tenero, making use of traffic-free paved paths throughout (though pedestrians have to vie for space with the many cyclists who also enjoy using the route). Along the way there are plenty of opportunities for eating and drinking – or for just marvelling at the lake's glistening surface and watching boats bob into and out of the many small harbours.

ACCESS

Delta Maggia bus stop is at the end of the #3 local bus route (from Locarno station). Frequent trains and buses connect Tenero station with Locarno.

The walk begins outside the entrance to Locarno's largest camp site. ▶ Heading N along the road, within a minute you'll pass by the entrance (R) to the **Parco delle Camelie** (Park of the Camellias).

> The entrance to the **Parco delle Camelie** (open daily throughout the year) is easy to miss as it's shared with the entrance to the Lake View Beach and Lounge Bar. The park was inaugurated in 2005 and is planted with 850 varieties of camellias, whose flowers are typically red or pink in colour; the plants have their origin in East and Southeast Asia.

A minute's walk further on you'll see a sculpture over to the R which is the most prominent feature of the **Parco della Pace** (Peace Park).

> The **Parco della Pace** was established in 1965 on the fortieth anniversary of the signing of the Locarno

This is the southern end of the delta of the River Maggia, a semi-circle of land that sticks out into the lake over which Locarno and Ascona spread.

The lakefront at Locarno, along which the walk runs

Pact, one of the most important treaties signed in Europe between the two world wars. The sculpture, of a bound man, remembers the Assyrian genocide of 1915, when over a quarter of a million Syriac Christians were slaughtered or deported by Ottoman troops in what is now southeast Turkey, northern Syria and northwestern Iraq (although the Turkish government has disputed labelling it a 'genocide').

Keep on N along the road, past the knot of water slides outside the lido on the R and the entrance to a sports stadium on the L, to come to (R) the oval-shaped **Hans Arp Sculpture Park** (10 min from the start of the walk).

Hans (Jean) Arp (1886–1966) was a German–French sculptor, painter and poet. A leading figure in the avant-garde, Zurich-based Dadaist movement, he sought exile in Switzerland during the war and is buried in Locarno's cemetery. A selection of his abstract, curving sculptures can be seen in the park.

There's an information board about the life and work of Hans Arp here.

Walk through the park to the paved footpath beside the harbour. ◄ Head N past the ice-cream parlours and cafes and through the **Giardino Pubblico** (Public Gardens; 10 min from the sculpture park – the train station is a block to the N) and past a children's play area to another small harbour, which marks the start of the dedicated pedestrian and cycle way along the lake, linking Locarno and Tenero. After 5 min the stone belltower of the sixteenth century **Chiesa San Quirico** rises on the L – access is a couple of min further on (past some public toilets) via a subway under the railway line.

There are some rather faded medieval frescoes on the interior walls of the **church** – the oldest are on the south wall and date from the thirteenth century, showing scenes from the life of Jesus. The freestanding belltower has medieval origins and once served as a watchtower. The gardens, shaded by grape vines, make for a cool rest stop on a hot day.

Carry on along the path, past some low-key beaches for sunbathing and swimming, and after 5–10 min you'll pass the **Cà di Ferro**. ▶ A minute's walk further on is the uber-stylish **Giardino Lago** restaurant and hotel.

After another 20 min you reach the outskirts of **Tenero**. Ignore the busy road underpass (L) and take the path that skirts a small parking area, turning R and then L outside the L'Approdo di Mappo restaurant. Unfortunately this last part of the walk through Tenero runs through a rather humdrum area of apartment blocks, pedestrian underpasses and sports facilities. Immediately beyond the **Centro Sportivo Minusio** (adjacent to the restaurant), take the pedestrian underpass (L) under the motorway (shared with a watercourse), a few steps after which you should turn L under the railway line. An immediate R turn here and a 5-min walk along a path that runs alongside the railway line brings you to **Tenero Station**, the walk's terminus.

In the sixteenth century this building served as a barracks for mercenary troops. It's now a private residence.

WALK 11

Sentiero Collina Alta and Sentiero Collina Bassa

Start/finish	Top station of the Funicolare Madonna del Sasso
Distance	13.5km (8.5 miles)
Ascent/descent	440m
Difficulty	Grade 2
Walking time	4 hr
Terrain	Easy forest paths and metalled minor roads throughout
Refreshments	There are eating options in Contra (half-way) and in Brione, on the way back – and a very pleasant café can also be found across the road from the funicular's top station. Buy snacks and drinks from the shops by Locarno train station (open 7 days) before heading for the funicular.

When the rainclouds start to curl in over Lake Maggiore – and you will be very lucky if they don't, if you spend a few days in the town – high-level walks in the surrounding mountains become less appealing. The walk described here, however, makes for a good option in poor weather, never rising higher than the 650m contour and rarely straying far from shelter and settlement. Starting from the top station of Locarno's funicular railway, which sits next to a fine monastery church, the walk makes use of two marked routeways that link Locarno with the village of Contra, to the east – heading out via the high (*alta*) route and back via the low (*bassa*) route. The former runs through thick forest while the latter makes use of back roads that link a string of modern settlements above Locarno. Both paths run along the valley flanks that drop down to the lake shore, and allow for fabulous views over the eastern arm of the lake and beyond, to the Monte Tamaro massif.

ACCESS

The Funicolare Madonna del Sasso operates daily throughout the year (though beware possible maintenance closures during November) from a base station at Viale Francesco Balli 2, 120m from the main railway station in Locarno along the main street into the town centre. The top station is also reachable on local bus (#2) from Locarno station, or there's a chapel-lined path up (20 min) which passes through the scenic defile in the rock cut by the Torrente Ramogno.

From the top station of the **funicular** head R (with the lake behind you) along Via Santuario. After less than 5 min turn L up a narrow lane, the Sentiero al Calvario, which after just 1 min becomes a flight of steps. These steps flatten out onto a high terrace; however, you'll soon find yourself on more steps that bring you up to another road, the Via Patocchi (10 min from the funicular station). Turn L and walk along the road for 5–10 min to a track sign pointing R along the Sentiero del Rocolo. After a few metres the signs will point you R into the trees. Ignore the track junction 100m later and keep heading along the marked Via Eco, slowly climbing up through woodland.

A view over Locarno from the first part of the walk

After 10 min you'll cross the **Verigana river** on a foot-bridge, and 10 min later you'll emerge onto another road, the Mulattiera San Bernardo, beside some houses.

Taking directions from the track marker post here (to Ronco and Tenero FFS) you need to head up the Mulattiera San Bernardo, though after just 3 min you're signposted back into the trees. From here there's an uneventful 30 min level walk through trees followed by a 10-min walk along a minor road, after which you turn R off the road and head back down into the trees. Five minutes beyond the junction you'll see the shell of a **ruined chapel** just off the path, down to the R.

> The **chapel** dates from the seventeenth century and was built on a pilgrimage route. However, an outbreak of the plague meant that it was destined never to be completed. Its history is told in English on an information board.

Just 3 min beyond the chapel later the path crosses the '**Roman Bridge**', an elegant arched bridge over the Navegna torrent. ▶ Beyond the bridge the path brings you after 10 min onto a metalled road. Heading along this road, after 5 min look out for the sign at a hairpin bend directing you back into the trees. After barely a few steps you have to turn R on a path that leads down to another track junction (indicating Contra).

The path drops down through trees onto a road; turn L here and in 5 min you'll be in the small village of **Contra**. You'll see the **Ristorante San Bernardino** to the L as the road threads through the village – a good place for a half-way stop (reached after 2 hours from the start point). ▶ Head on past the restaurant for the next track marker post, which points R (to Tenero FFS), leading you between the village's church and Casa Communale. Yellow diamonds painted onto walls and pavements now take over as you are led down narrow lanes and flights of steps which eventually bring you out after 20 min at the **Oratorio della Fraccia**.

> The **Oratorio della Fraccia** is a Baroque church that offers a superb view of the lake from its graceful arched portico, which dates from the decades either side of 1700. If you find the church open, check out the interior's marble balustrade, the elegant stucco work and the ornate canvases – all from the eighteenth century.

From the church, continue on down the flight of steps until you meet a minor road, where a sign on a gatepost points R to the hamlet of Mondacce. After just a few steps this road brings you out on the Via Contra, a main road which you must head up for 5 min until you reach the centre of **Mondacce** itself, where a track marker post by a water fountain indicates the Sentiero Collina Bassa. After heading just a few steps in the direction indicated bear R onto the cobbled lane that diverges from the paved road. In a couple of moments you reach another set of steps which are again signed the Sentiero Collina Bassa. The

The name of the Roman Bridge is misleading as, according to the information board next to it, the structure only dates to 1750.

There are direct buses down to Locarno (#312), and to the train station at Tenero, from the Contra Paese bus stop outside the restaurant.

A view over the Madonna del Sasso monastery from the end of the walk

steps constitute the start of the Alle Selve, which joins a road, the Via Mondacce, in just a couple of minutes. Another couple of minutes further on you follow the sign R off the road and onto a path that rises through the trees.

This path includes the only tricky scrambling you have to do on this walk – over a couple of slabs of rock – but you are soon back on a metalled road, the Via Albaredo. From now on, the path rarely takes you off metalled roads – making progress swift. Some 15 min after joining the Via Albaredo there's a L turn onto the Via Panoramica, which bypasses the small village of **Brione**, running below and parallel to the main road through the village. ◄ Beyond Brione the Via Panoramica becomes a footpath as it drops down to cross the **River Rabissale** in a wooded glade. Rising to a parking area with some garages, you find yourself once again on a metalled road – this time, the Via Caselle – which brings you after 10 min to a junction with the Via Consiglio Mezzano. Turning R here brings you onto Via Santuario – with

There are a couple of low-key places in Brione serving and selling food: to reach them stay on the Via Brione at the Via Panoramica turn-off.

wonderful views over the **Madonna del Sasso** monastery – and the funicular station, reached after just a couple of minutes from the junction.

MADONNA DEL SASSO MONASTERY CHURCH

The pastel-hued Madonna del Sasso (Our Lady of the Rock) is the most prominent monastery-church in Ticino. It was founded after an apparition of the Virgin Mary appeared to a monk in 1480. The photogenic complex (open daily, 7am–6.30pm) includes a number of graceful porticos while the terraces provide great views over the lake. The church itself contains a number of valuable paintings including The Flight into Egypt by Bramantino (circa 1520). It can be accessed via a short walk down from the funicular top station, though there is also a designated part-way station serving it.

WALK 12
Cimetta to Mergoscia via Capanna dei Monti di Lego

Start	Top station of Cimetta chairlift
Finish	Mergoscia Posta bus stop
Distance	11.75km (7.25 miles)
Ascent	350m
Descent	1260m
Difficulty	Grade 2
Walking time	4 hr 15 min
Terrain	Forest and well-maintained mountain paths; metalled roads at end
Refreshments	The café by the Cimetta chairlift base station, and the Capanna dei Monti di Lego, serve refreshments.

With the funicular railway, cable car and chairlift whisking you with ease to an altitude of 1671m above Locarno, this route allows for some high-altitude walking amidst fantastic scenery without too many uphill sections;

paths are well-graded in terms of steepness and are easily accessible, even for families with older children. The views over Lake Maggiore, Locarno and the Verzasca valley are breathtaking – but choose a fine day as the first part of the walk is along exposed mountain ridges (guiding you to the summit of Cima della Trosa) before the route plunges into the forested slopes of the Val Verzasca. The convivial Capanna dei Monti di Lego, situated in a forest clearing with views over Locarno, provides an excellent pit-stop towards the end of the walk.

ACCESS

See under Walk 11 for details of Locarno's Funicolare Madonna del Sasso, whose base station is near Locarno railway station. From its top station take the cable car to Cardada, then walk 5 min along a paved track for the base station of the chairlift to Cimetta. Coming back, the #B312 bus runs from Mergoscia Posta to Locarno railway station every 1–2 hours (journey time 33 min).

Take the path that drops down from behind the top station of the **Cimetta** chairlift. Almost immediately, turn R onto a well-maintained stony path, which in less than 5 min brings you down to a track marker post with Cima della Trosa signed. From here a well-graded path rises towards the peak, with stunning views of Lake Maggiore and the surrounding valleys opening up. After 35 min a sign points the way to the summit of **Cima della Trosa** (1869m), reached in less than 5 min. The rocky summit is marked by a large cross. It's exposed but easily accessible, with some scrambling over boulders right at the top.

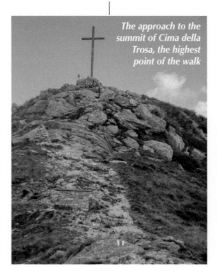

The approach to the summit of Cima della Trosa, the highest point of the walk

From the summit, retrace your steps to the track marker post (less than 5 min) and take the route sign-posted Mergoscia and Monti di Lego. After just 2 min turn L and follow the track down from the exposed ridge onto high pastureland. After 20 min there's a marker post situated on a high ridge. ◄ From the ridge head down towards the cluster of farm buildings, reached after 25 min. Monti di Lego is now signed, the path taking you through the farm buildings and into the forest on a route marked both by red-and-white stripes and by red patches on trees.

The path now undulates along the forested ridge. Some 15 min from the farm buildings there's a L turn at a junction, with Monti di Lego signed on a rock. There's an uphill section now, which levels off and it followed by a downhill section, bringing you to a viewpoint (with a bench) overlooking the lakeside resort of Tenero (1 hour from the junction). Just 5 min later you'll reach a cluster of stone buildings in a clearing – Monti di Lego – and, in another 5 min, the **Capanna dei Monti di Lego** itself, a low stone building that's clearly signed. ◄

From the *capanna* take the path signed Mergoscia. This is a well-graded and maintained forest path, with fences and steps in places. You'll soon see the village through the trees, spread out picturesquely across south-facing slopes. After an hour the path becomes a paved lane which leads to a parking area at **Busada** which is the western extension of Mergoscia. From the parking area follow the metalled road through the village until it meets the main road at a T junction; turn L here and follow the road up to the village church in **Mergoscia**. The post office and bus stop are in the adjacent square (15 min from the parking area).

This is a good place to rest up, with views dropping away into the Val Versasca on one side and the Valle Maggia on the other.

This is a great stop for refreshments, either at the capanna itself or on the grass that rises beside it to the fantastic viewpoint by the small chapel.

WALK 13
The Centovalli from Camedo to Intragna

Start	Camedo railway station
Finish	Intragna railway station
Distance	10.5km (6.5 miles)
Ascent	500m
Descent	700m
Difficulty	Grade 2
Walking time	4 hr
Terrain	Woodland paths predominate, with some vehicle tracks and metalled roads
Refreshments	Nowhere along the route sells or serves food; stock up on snacks and drinks in the small supermarket beside Locarno station before you set off.

The Centovalli – literally, 'a hundred valleys' – is a narrowing cleft in the mountains that stretches west from the village of Intragna (itself just west of Locarno) to the Italian border at Camedo. It's a highly scenic landscape of frothing waterfalls and thick chestnut forests, with traditional stone-built villages clinging to its upper slopes. The valley is served by trains on the narrow gauge Centovalli railway (see box below), which gives access to both the start and end points of this walk. In former times villagers hereabouts would bring their produce to Locarno's market by mule, and over the centuries a mule track, carefully engineered in places with embankments and bridges, was established for this purpose. The mule track – the Via del Mercato – was eventually superseded by the main road that now runs through the bottom of the valley, but today this high-level route which links valley-side villages is popular with walkers. The scenery along the walk is ever-changing and because it follows the former mule track (and, in its lower stages, metalled roads) it is never difficult underfoot. There are a couple of steep uphill sections, but for much of the way you'll find yourself walking on a gently downhill gradient. The route does not go higher than 840m, so is walkable for much of the year.

ACCESS

Both Camedo and Intragna are stations on the Centovalli rail line (see box).

THE CENTOVALLI RAILWAY

The Centovalli railway (vigezzinacentovalli.com) – properly the Domodossola–Locarno railway, informally called Vigezzina in Italy and Centovallina in Switzerland – connects Locarno with the town of Domodossola in the Italian Alps. It's a metre-gauge line and one of the most scenic in Ticino, with trains squealing round tight curves and crossing multiple viaducts on the two-hour journey (the border at Camedo is reached after just 40 minutes). The railway opened in 1923; the terminus was originally west of Locarno's centre but a tunnel was later built under the streets of the city and today trains operate from an underground terminus at Locarno's main railway station.

You'll see a track marker post, pointing the way to Intragna, right by the platform at **Camedo station**. Head up the steps to the road, turn R and follow it round a hairpin to a T junction. Turn left and after a few steps you'll see a track signpost pointing R, along the Via San Lorenzo, which will take you up through the heart of the village of **Camedo**. Once you emerge from the lane onto a road, head L – the markers will send you R almost immediately, up to a higher part of the same road. Turn R and head up the road, looking for the marker post on the L that sends you up above the road, cutting off one of the hairpin bends.

The route now takes you across the road and into the centre of the village of **Borgnone**. Follow the marker signs around the church and up onto the road once more: heading along the road you reach (R) an information board about the Via Mercato and a sign pointing you R, down past a small chapel and on into the trees (20 min from Camedo). This is the start of the Via del Mercato 'proper'.

In the village of Verdasio

Verdasio makes for a very pleasant place to stop – with a handy bench outside the church, and a good view from the church's terrace. Unfortunately there's no café here.

For a short while the path hugs the road (though is just below it) and passes the ruins of a **former ironworks**. Beyond these the route makes use of boardwalks and footbridges, and passes (20 min from the information board) a small chapel. Thirty minutes later you cross an unusual, green-coloured pedestrian **girder bridge** before following the route steeply up through trees to reach the village of **Verdasio** some 15 min later. ◄

From the church in Verdasio follow the signs up through the village and back into the trees: this is by far the most strenuous ascent of the walk. After 15 min another marker post marks the top of the climb, and soon after you drop down steeply to ford a gushing river. Beyond the ford the route rises again (though not as steeply or as far as the descent) to a level path. After another 20 min you arrive at some farm buildings: the route runs up beside them to a marker post, pointing you R. Within half an hour you pass what looks to be some low-key hydro-electric power facilities beside a gushing waterfall, immediately beyond which the route becomes a vehicle track and then a metalled road.

Some 20 min after becoming a road a track marker post at a road junction points the way to Intragna. Just 2 min later another marker post is reached, this time with two ways to Intragna marked. Taking the route that drops down rather than stays on the level, just over 5 min later you reach a road, where you should turn L. After only 2 min another track marker gives two options for reaching Intragna. The shorter duration route (30 min) sends you down on stepped paths through a scattering of houses that mark the outskirts of **Intragna**.

The stepped paths lead to a main road. Cross it and look for the path that leads on down to a pedestrian level crossing over the Centovalli railway line. This route runs through an attractive part of Intragna before re-crossing the railway line on another pedestrian level crossing. A lane takes you up to a road, which you should follow for just a few steps until 'Piazza Stazione' is signposted to the R. Following this route takes you down to Intragna station in just a minute or so.

The walk runs through lush woodland, crossing many rivers

WALK 14
The Valle del Salto

Start/finish	Maggia Centro bus stop
Distance	8km (5 miles)
Ascent/descent	640m
Difficulty	Grade 2
Walking time	3 hr 30 min
Terrain	Woodland paths predominate (steep in places), with some metalled lanes
Refreshments	The Migros supermarket opposite the bus stop will supply you with any snacks and water you might need, though it's closed on Sunday and watch out for its noon–2pm closure Mon–Sat. The walk also passes a couple of atmospheric cafes in Maggia's attractive old quarter.

The Valle del Salto is a dramatic side valley that cuts northeast from the main Valle Maggia at the town of Maggia, less than half an hour by bus from Locarno. This circular walk along the flanks of the Valle de Salto takes in a number of small chapels, not to mention crossing chasm-like gorges whose gushing torrents are spanned by footbridges, as it leads walkers along the valley's northwest flank and then back to Maggia along the southeast flank, affording constantly changing views over the valley at every turn. There's a fair amount of ascent to do (mostly on stone staircases that rise up through the forest) but the walk's maximum altitude is 880m, meaning that it's walkable for much of the year (it's particularly attractive on a sunny day in Autumn, when the light catches the myriad colours of the changing leaves). It's also a very popular walk – partly because although this attractive valley is very accessible from Locarno it is twisting and thickly forested, with a real feel of isolation about it for walkers.

ACCESS
Maggia Centro is on bus route #315 from Locarno to Bignasco and Cavergno (hourly; 25 min journey time).

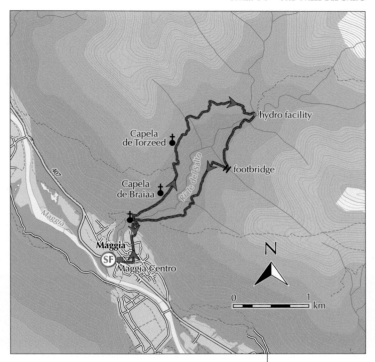

The track marker post at the bus stop points the way to the 'Giro Valle del Salto', sending you first into the heart of the handsome old town of **Maggia**, which spreads across the east bank of the river, firmly bypassed by the main road. After barely a couple of minutes signs at the cobbled Piazza del Pózz will send you N along La Gesgiòla, which winds its way past the town's main church. Some 200m further on you need to make a R turn, still following the signs to the Valle del Salto; a flight of steps brings you up to a **chapel** (reached after 20 min from the bus stop) and some fine views over the town and the Valle Maggia. This is the start of the circular walk: signs outside the chapel indicate that both the path heading N and that heading E, up the hill, will lead you through the Valle del Salto: the usual way of doing the walk is to now head N, making for the Capèla de Braiaa and almost immediately crossing a torrent via a footbridge that spans a deep chasm.

There's around 50 min of climbing to do now, as the route ascends the northwestern flank of the valley, passing the **Capèla de Braiaa** and a second chapel, the **Capèla de Torzéed**, before levelling off to become a ridgeside path that must in former times have been a mule track. Some 45 min later you round the head of the valley and drop steeply down through the trees to reach an intriguing **hydro facility** located in a deep rocky glade – and a track marker post indicating the way back to Maggia.

The main highlight on the return journey comes after another 25 min and comprises the traversing of a sloping metal **footbridge** that takes you down over another raging torrent, and then on along the side of the cliff: a cable attached to the cliffside is provided to help you navigate

The routes around the Valle de Salto divide outside this chapel

this part, although you are also separated from the chasm by a fence. Things are less eventful after this, with the path affording great views over the valley's northeastern flanks – where you were walking an hour or so ago.

Some 50 min beyond the footbridge you'll find yourself once more on the outskirts of **Maggia**, heading down to the **chapel** above the town from where you simply retrace your steps to the bus stop (reached after another 20 min).

WALK 15

Along the Val Lavizzara from Fusio to Bignasco

Start	Fusio Paese bus stop
Finish	Bignasco Posta bus stop
Distance	17.75km (11 miles)
Ascent	360m
Descent	1210m
Difficulty	Grade 2
Walking time	5 hr 15 min
Terrain	Forest paths predominate, with some vehicle tracks and metalled roads
Refreshments	There are no shops in any of the villages the walk passes through. There are places serving food and drink in Fusio, Prato, Peccia and Bignasco.

Towering walls of rock, deep chasms filled with tumbling torrents and traditional stone-built villages clinging to steep mountain terraces characterize the long and often lonely Val Lavizzara, the name given to the valley of the River Maggia between Bignasco and Fusio. Along its length the valley is watched over by the stubborn, brooding massif of the Piz Campo Tencia. The walk presented here runs the whole length of the Val Lavizzara, taking walkers through woods and across pastureland, sticking to the valley bottom all the way and very often hugging the banks of the swift-flowing Maggia as it grows from a bubbling mountain stream to a fully-fledged river. Conditions are rarely difficult underfoot and the designation of the walk as difficulty 2 comes largely from its length rather than the challenge of the terrain. Frequent access to the main road also means that it's very easy to shorten the walk, as bus stops are rarely far away. The walk's undoubted highlight is the church at Mogno, reached after just 30 min, a masterpiece of contemporary architecture in a stunning setting and one of the most striking buildings in the whole of Ticino – though in terms of scenery the most memorable part of the walk comes towards the end, where the sheer mountain walls close in as the river approaches Bignasco through a dramatic gorge.

ACCESS

Hourly buses run from Locarno to Bignasco Posta (journey time 50 min) where you need to change onto a bus for Fusio (4–5 daily, 40–50 min journey time).

It's just a few steps from the bus stop to the Hotel Fusio, whose café-restaurant is often packed out with walkers. Fusio's village centre lies just beyond.

The bus will drop you at the only bus stop in **Fusio**, where a veritable forest of track walking signs seem to spout beside the fast-flowing Maggia. ◀ At the marker post pick up the signs for Bignasco and follow the metalled minor road as it rises up past the church and to the L of the Pineta Restaurant.

The **Pineta Restaurant** is open from 3pm Tues–Sat. There are fine views from the path by the restaurant across to the pastel-coloured houses of Fusio, which look as if they are about to slide down the steep valley sides and into the waters of the Maggia! This is undoubtedly one of the most photogenic villages in the Locarno valleys.

Beyond the restaurant the road quickly becomes a grassy lane that guides you down and onto a vehicle track that runs through trees along the flanks of the valley. After 20 min watch out for the short cut that leads you steeply down through the forest for a short distance, cutting off a hairpin bend. Turning left as the path rejoins the road, you soon reach the houses of the small village of **Mogno**,

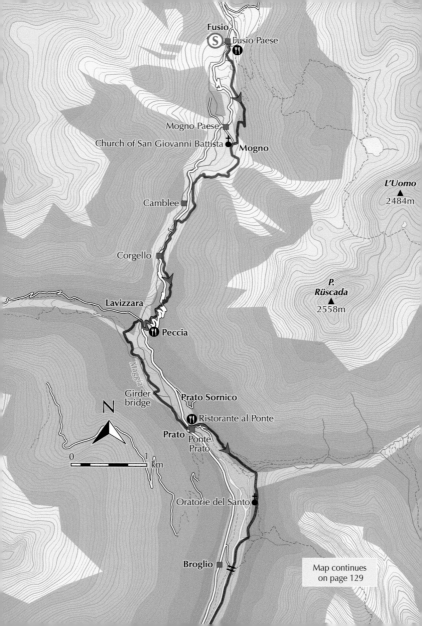

Fusio

S

Fusio Paese

Mogno Paese

Church of San Giovanni Battista

Mogno

L'Uomo
▲
2484m

Camblee

Corgello

P.
Rüscada
▲
2558m

Lavizzara

Peccia

Girder
bridge

Prato Sornico

Ristorante al Ponte

Prato

Ponte
Prato

N

0   1
km

Oratorie del Santo

Broglio

Map continues
on page 129

THE CHURCH OF SAN GIOVANNI BATTISTA AT MOGNO

The remarkable church at Mogno is one of the highlights of the walk

The Church of San Giovanni Battista (St John the Baptist) at Mogno was constructed between 1994 and 1996 on the site of an older church (from 1626), which was levelled by an avalanche in 1986. The new church was designed by famed Ticino architect Mario Botta (born 1943), who has designed many buildings in Switzerland and across the world (such as the San Francisco Museum of Modern Art). The starkly modernist design uses alternating layers of pale marble and grey granite (both quarried locally) to stunning effect: it's a building not to be missed. Note that it's a 200m walk (along the road) from the church to the main road that runs along the valley bottom, where there are public toilets and a bus stop (Mogno Paese).

Be sure to look over your shoulder here for views back over Mogno, beautifully cradled by the valley sides and the mountains beyond.

and the curved back of the village's **church** will hove into view – one of the most remarkable sights in Ticino.

The route continues along the lane that runs behind the church. This soon becomes a vehicle track. ◄ After a walk along the level terrace the path drops down to a lane (around 20 min after leaving Mogno). **Camblee** bus stop is just a minute's walk to the R, but the route

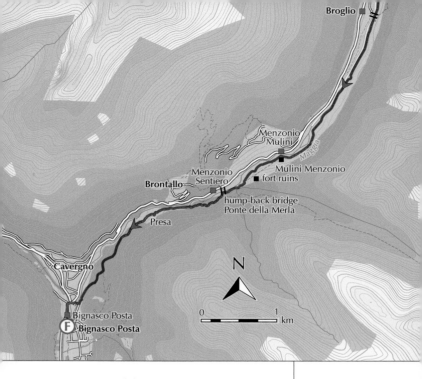

continues L up the hill (signposted to Peccia). After just 10 min you reach the main road, which you need to walk along for around 5–10 min before being signposted L up a lane just before the Corgello bus stop. Ten minutes later you begin the steep descent into Peccia – keep a careful watch out for the markers as the path and the road (descending via a series of hairpins) intertwine here.

After 20 min you'll be walking along the road through the centre of **Peccia**. ▶ Turn R at the Reifeisen bank onto a side road, walk past the parking places and follow the road as it swings L over a bridge. Immediately after the bridge a marker post points you L, to Bignasco and Prato Sornico. Just 10 min later a track marker post points you L; the next 20 min is through woodland beside the fast-flowing Maggia river.

Peccia is not particularly appealing but there's a bus stop here and an osteria, the Medici (closed Sat), whose front door the route passes.

There's another restaurant here, the Ristorante al Ponte (closed Mon and Tues), right beside the bridge, and a bus stop – Ponte Prato.

Reaching a picnic site on the outskirts of the bland village of Prato Sornico (which you do not need to enter, but where there's another bus stop) you'll be directed R across a pedestrian girder bridge and then L along a path that clings to the west bank of the river. After 10 min you arrive at a bridge that carries the main road across the river just outside the village of **Prato**. ◄

Prato has a more genuinely rustic feel to it than Peccia. You're directed along the main street and then back into the woods. After 20 min you cross a venerable hump-backed pedestrian bridge that spans a deep chasm, and just 5–10 min later you arrive at the **Oratorie del Santo**, a small chapel with a pastel-pink façade that sits amidst a tight cluster of dwellings.

Some 10 min later the path drops down onto a metalled road: there's a bridge over an impressive cascade here and 5–10 min later there's access, via a modern pedestrian bridge over the Maggia, to **Broglio** bus stop on the main road. The metalled road now allows for swift progress through lush pastureland – but 20 min beyond the pedestrian bridge the route becomes a muddy path through the trees once more, and there's another pedestrian bridge across the Maggia, at **Mulini Menzonio** – this one giving access to Menzonio Mulini bus stop on the main road.

Some 15 min beyond Mulini Menzonio the path passes an intriguing concrete **fort** dug into the wooded hillside. ◄ Immediately beyond the fort there's a steep drop down through the trees to a pedestrian suspension bridge that spans a cascading torrent – this bridge being the type that bounces alarmingly under your feet as you cross it! Five minutes later you pass another of the beautiful and venerable **hump-back bridges** which distinguish the valley – this one, named Ponte della Merla, leads across the Maggia to the bus stop on the main road at Sentiero Menzonio. It's worth admiring the Maggia from the crest of the bridge, but the route doesn't require you to cross it: instead, continue on along the path that clings to the valley's eastern flanks, crossing (20 min beyond the bridge) a small tributary of the Maggia by means of

The fort was part of the defences built in the 1940s to disrupt any German invasion that might have taken place along this valley.

stepping stones before passing through the tiny, slope-clinging community of **Presa**.

Now you're definitely on the home straight of this long but rewarding walk: 15 min beyond Presa the path brings you out of the trees and along a terrace above Cavergno, Bignasco's northern extension, set right where the Valle Bavona meets the Val Lavizzara to form the Valle Maggia. Just 10–15 min later the signs direct you across the modern, stone-built bridge across the Maggia and into **Bignasco**. ▶ After crossing the Bavona the bus stop (and post office) is just a minute or further on to the south (L), along the main road.

Bignasco, at the end of the walk

Just beyond the bridge is the Albergo Hotel Posta, on whose terrace – overlooking the River Bavona – you can reward yourself with a fortifying drink.

131

WALK 16
Capanna Cristallina from Robiei

Start/finish	Upper station of San Carlo-Robiei cable car
Distance	12km (7.5 miles)
Ascent/descent	770m
Difficulty	Grade 3
Walking time	4 hr
Terrain	Metalled roads and mountain paths, challenging in places with some snow patches to cross even in summer
Refreshments	There are two cafés 5 min on foot from the upper cable car station at Robiei: the Albergo Robiei (the obvious octagonal high-rise building) and the more traditional Capanna Basòdino (take the metalled road running down from the cable car station; the *capanna* is hidden behind a rocky bluff). There are also refreshments available at the Capanna Cristallina, the walk's destination.

The Cristallina Massif divides the Val Bavona, an upper tributary valley of the Valle Maggia, from the Val Bedretto in the very northwest of Ticino (covered in part four of this book). It's a wild area of desolate but spectacular scenery, of plunging ravines and jewel-like lakes, all of it overlooked by the Basòdino glacier, a glimmering necklace of white that adorns the upper slopes of the Kastelhorn (3128m) and the Basòdino (3273m) on the Italian border. As far as walkers are concerned its focal point is Robiei, a sunny ledge reached by cable car from San Carlo at the head of the Val Bavona. It's a popular excursion – there are two restaurants there – and it forms the start and end point of a challenging walk to one of Ticino's most spectacularly-situated mountain huts, the Capanna Cristallina, perched on a ledge at the top of the Cristallina Pass which divides the Bavona and Bedretto valleys. The *capanna* can also be visited on a longer walk from the Bedretto valley (see Walk 33) and indeed it is easy to combine the walk described here with that walk, perhaps using the Capanna Cristallina for an overnight stay.

ACCESS

Bus #315 from Locarno station to Bignasco (hourly, 55 min) then bus #333 from Bignasco direct to Funivia San Carlo-Robiei (infrequent) or to San Carlo Ponte for a 650m walk to cable car base station (25 min journey time).

ROBIEI AND ITS CABLE CAR

The cable car to Robiei, built in 1972, is one of the most hair-raising in Switzerland: an enormous cabin capable of holding dozens of people at a time glides spectacularly above precipitous ravines and plunging cliffs, the cables suspended by sturdy pylons built in what look to be the most inaccessible locations. Robiei itself will come as a surprise to many – as it's an Alpine wonderland that's also an industrial hub: a hydro dam (holding back the Lago di Robiei) overlooks the plateau on which the cable car station is built, and the strange octagonal high-rise building (now a hostel) in front of it dates from the time of the dam's construction in the 1960s when it was built as workers' accommodation. Other dams in the surrounding valleys, all of them holding back reservoirs of snowmelt from the surrounding glaciers, can be seen on the walk. The existence of metalled roads at this altitude will also surprise many; there are often lorries trundling around and helicopters buzzing aloft, too.

The track marker post beneath the cable car station points the way to the *capanna* along a metalled road that rises steadily around the southern and eastern shores of the Lago di Robiei (the lake is invisible behind the dam and then behind a high ledge of rock). The road is well graded and leads you up into a classically spectacular high-alpine environment of tumbling streams and grassy summer pastureland. After 30 min a sign points R on a path leading up the hill.

The zig-zag ascent up the bare mountainside takes around 35 min, with steps in places but also some scrambling over exposed rocks. At the top of the ascent a track marker post sends you L along a more gradually-graded path that rises along the western side of an exposed ridge. Some 35 min from the marker post the

Pizzo Gararesc
2729m

Pizzo del Narè
2588m

Poncione della
Forca di
Cristallina
2792m

Capanna Cristallina

Ghiacciaio
di Valleggia

Poncione
di Vallegia
2873m

Cima
di Lago
2833m

Pizzo
Cristallina
2911m

Pizzo
andinagia
2774m

o Cavagnöö
2836m

Lago
Sfundau

ridge crest
2466m

aerial cableway
no public access

Lago dei
Cavagnöö

Pizzo del Ghiacciaio
di Sasso Nero
2842m

Lago
Nero

start of
mountain
path ascent

izzo dell'Arzo
2755m

Lago di
Robiei

Robiei

SF

Albergo
Robiei

Capanna
Basodino

Bavona

Poncione di Braga
2864m

Lago
del Zott

Pulpito
2616m

N

0   1
         km

hiacciaio
el Basodino

San Carlo

Bavona

path crests a ridge (2466m) and you will find yourself looking down on **Lago Sfundau**. ▸ Look due North from the crest and you will see the *capanna* perched high on a ridge. From the crest you need to drop down onto the path that now skirts the lake's eastern shore, running high above it on the valley side.

The path is well-made with ropes and steps at a couple of points, though there will also be some snow patches to cross. As you leave the lake behind, you embark on the final stage of the walk, a graded ascent of the south side of the Passo di Cristallina. The hut (2575m) is reached in just under an hour from the crest at the southern end of the lake.

The **capanna** (tel. 091 869 23 30; http://capanna cristallina.casticino.ch/) is a stylish building of wood, concrete, steel and stone that was built entirely from scratch in 2003, the previous huts on the pass (located in a slightly different position) having been destroyed by avalanches. The location,

The lake is in a bowl and is partly iced even in August.

The spectacular approach to Capanna Cristallina (seen at the top of the frame)

on a ridge between the Val Torta and the bowl in which the Sfundau lake is situated, is spectacular. The *capanna* serves basic refreshments and has 120 beds in 17 rooms and is open from the end of June to the beginning of October. From here Ossasco in the Val Bedretto (for bus services to Airolo) is reachable in 2 hr 30 min while Pesciüm (for the cable car down to Airolo) is 4 hours away – see Walk 33 for more details.

To return to Robiei, simply retrace your steps.

WALK 17

Bosco Gurin to Cimalmotto

Start	Top station of Bosco Gurin to Rossboda chairlift
Finish	Cimalmotto bus stop
Distance	6.5km (4 miles)
Ascent	240m
Descent	840m
Difficulty	Grade 2
Walking time	3 hr
Terrain	Mountain paths in first section, with chains and cables to guide in places, though no steep ascents; forest paths in second section, descending to metalled roads at the end
Refreshments	There's a small Co-op supermarket in Bosco Gurin (open Mon– Sat 9am [8.30am Sat]–noon and 3–6pm [5pm Sat, no afternoon openings Mon]). At the start of the walk, the Ristorante Rossboda in the upper chairlift station, or the more traditional Capanna Grossalp, 15 min away on foot, can provide refreshments. At the end of the walk, the Rifugio la Reggia is 15 min walk away from Cimalmotto bus stop on the hillside above the village (though check for opening days: www.dinodb.ch) – or walk 1km down the road from the bus stop to Locanda Fior di Campo (www.fiordicampo.ch) beside Campo Paese bus stop, which has a restaurant/café with a terrace.

The village of Bosco Gurin, accessed via a dramatic side valley from the Valle Maggia, is unique in two respects – it's the highest settlement in Ticino, and because of a quirk of history, its inhabitants have traditionally spoken German rather than Italian. It's a picturesque village of burnt-wood chalets set amidst some mightily grand scenery, which you can easily access via a chairlift that ascends the upper slopes of the great rocky bowl in which the village is situated. The walk described here circles this great bowl and then crosses over the Passo Quadrella, finishing up in the very different village of Cimalmotto in the neighbouring valley. Although there are some difficult sections on the path, the chairlift takes care of the bulk of the ascent – meaning that this walk gives access to some fabulous scenery without being too lengthy. However, you should plan your walk in advance: you need a clear day, the bus services to Bosco Gurin and (particularly) Cimalmotto are sparse, and neither the chairlift nor the eating options at Cimalmotto are open every day, even in midsummer.

ACCESS

Bus #315 from Locarno to Cevio (half-hourly; 45 min journey time) then bus #331 to Bosco Gurin (5 daily; 45 min journey time). The base station of the chairlift (check days of operation in advance on www.bosco-gurin.ch) is a 10-min walk from the bus stop in Bosco Gurin. From Cimalmotto there are only 3 daily buses to Cerentino (#Bus 332) for connection onto one of the Bosco Gurin to Cevio buses.

BOSCO GURIN

Bosco Gurin owes its unique linguistic heritage to the so-called Walser migrations of the Middle Ages, where the Walser people, who spoke a dialect of German, moved here from the upper parts of Canton Valais (Wallis in German). There are many suggested reasons for the move: it might have been because of disputes that Walser had with feudal overlords, it might have been because of problems with overpopulation in the Valais, or it might have been because the rulers of Locarno had a need for mercenary soldiers, and the tough Walser men fitted the bill as recruits. Settlers arrived in the valley in 1244 and since much of the land was already farmed, they were left with the pastures at its remotest, highest end – hence the village being located at such a high altitude (1500m). Isolation and out-migration have always been a problem and nowadays the village has a permanent population of only a few dozen, with Italian being the predominant language. However, a dialect of German is still spoken by a third of residents and the village's unique heritage is proudly celebrated by the Gothic script used on signs and by the small Walserhaus museum (open Tues–Sat 10–11.30am and 1.30–5m). Despite the tortuous road journey to get here the village is now a popular centre for walkers in summer and for skiers in winter.

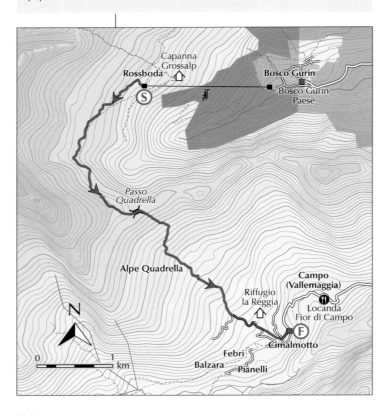

The track marker post outside the upper station of the chairlift points the way to Cimalmotto and the Passo Quadrella. The path initially hugs the contours, running under the cables of a ski lift, but then begins to climb as it circles the great bowl in the mountainside that cradles Bosco Gurin, reaching a mini-summit on a ridge with a cairn after 30 min. After this the path becomes more challenging as it rises up to the pass, with chains and cables fixed to the rock in places. There are great views back over Bosco Gurin and the chairlift station as the path ascends the pass – while the ridge towering above you to the W marks the border with Italy. The summit of the **Passo Quadrella** (2137m), with its cairn, is reached 1 hr 10 min from the chairlift station.

Coming down from the pass, a track marker post reached 5–10 min from the summit points you to Cimalmotto down a path that drops steeply into the trees. ▶ After 45 min descending through the trees you reach a cluster of buildings at **Alpe Quadrella**; 35 min further on (along more gently graded paths) you emerge

The cable car station at Rossboda marks the start of the walk

The scattered dwellings of the neighbouring villages of Cimalmotto and Campo are now clearly visible on the valley floor below.

139

A distant view of the chairlift station at Rossboda, which is the start of this walk

from the forest onto a metalled road which curls around the uppermost houses of **Cimalmotto**.

Head down the road into the village. ◄ After 5–10 min walking along the road into the village (assuming you haven't turned off for the *rifugio*) a sign directs you past a cross across meadowland on a short cut to the village church. At the church turn L and walk down the metalled road to the car park and bus stop at the lower end of the village (20 min from reaching the metalled road).

After 120m a road turns off L to the Rifugio la Reggia (see refreshments, above) – it's on the hillside below you after 300m.

WALK 18
Sentiero per l'Arte

Start	Ganne bus stop
Finish	Lavertezzo Paese bus stop
Distance	4.5km (3 miles)
Ascent	Negligible
Descent	130m
Difficulty	Grade 1
Walking time	1 hr 20 min
Terrain	Very easy woodland paths throughout, with no gradients
Refreshments	Although you can cross the river to the *osteria* at Motta around a third of the way in, there are no shops or eating places directly en route: stock up on food and drink before boarding the bus in Locarno.

This unusual route hugs the churning Verzasca river, which flows into Lake Maggiore just east of Locarno. The route is well-marked and easy to navigate and sticks closely to the thickly wooded west bank of the river, while the road to Sonogno, at the head of the Verzasca valley, runs along the opposite bank. In 1997 this section of the 25km path that runs from Sonogno all the way to Lake Maggiore was designated *un sentiero per l'arte* and some twenty contemporary art works were commissioned to line it. Over time some of the works have been removed or have simply disintegrated into the damp earth, but many remain – though plaques attributing and explaining the works have faded to illegibility (and tourist offices rarely stock the walk's now rather dated explanatory booklet). However, those works that do remain form an interesting accompaniment to an undemanding, gently downhill route that leads pleasantly through woods and across open stretches of pastureland. It's easy to combine this walk with Walk 19: the two together make a good circular walk from Lavertezzo, though you will miss the first part of the Sentiero per l'Arte if you combine them in this way.

ACCESS

Both Lavertezzo and Ganne are on the #321 bus route. Some buses run direct from Locarno; otherwise take a train from Locarno to Tenero (5 min journey time) and pick up the bus from there. Buses from Tenero run every 60–90 minutes (less frequently from Locarno). Journey times from Tenero are 29 min (Lavertezzo) and 39 min (Ganne).

Ganne itself is little more than a couple of houses beside a bend in the road. The route plunges into the forest at the small car park (and adjacent bus stop) situated on the L side of the road immediately after it crosses the Verzasca river. The first artwork – a bold column constructed from differently coloured and textured surfaces – hoves into

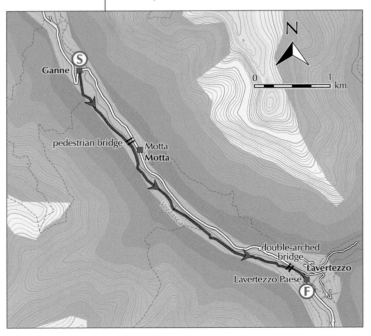

view after just 5 min. ▶ Some 3 min later the route crosses a tributary of the Verzasca on a wooden bridge that features some thin stainless steel viewing tubes that are the work of German physicist and artist Helmut Eigenmann. A few steps further on the Swiss sculptor Piero Tedoldi has incised the rocks around another wooden bridge with yellow streaks that resemble gashes or wounds; softer on the eye are the half-collapsed towers built of recycled wood and supported by trees that rise up to the right of the path a little further on – the work of a Ticino stage designer and artist named Gerardo Wuthier.

Fifteen minutes further on you'll see a **pedestrian bridge** spanning the river. ▶ Unless you are heading across to **Motta** there's no need to cross the bridge. Instead, stay on the path as it carries on along the west bank of the river.

The work of a German sculptor, Josef Briechle, the column's rough materials are a deliberate reference to the region's rural culture.

Crossing the bridge and turning R will bring you after 150m to Motta, which has a roadside Osteria (and adjacent bus stop) that marks the end of Walk 19.

Lavertezzo, at the end of the walk

143

The pyramid is the work of another Ticino artist, Antonio Lüönd; his work is inspired by the traditional spiritual and healing qualities associated with pyramids.

After just a few steps you'll see a pyramid built over a rock stranded in a field to the R of the path. ◀ Another 15 min will bring you to a work consisting of blue rectangles nestling amidst trees close to the river bank, the work of Swiss sculptor Ernesto Oescger. Immediately beyond this a gushing tributary of the Verzasca has to be navigated by means of narrow wooden bridges and stepping stones – a challenge for dogs or young children.

Two final works are visible on the final half hour of the walk, and both are fashioned from steel: a set of shields adorn a sheer cliff face on your R and, just 5 min further on, a set of abstract designs cover a rock to the L – the work of, respectively, the Swiss sculptor Rudolf Tschudin and the British land artist Sandra Eades.

The origins of the bridge lie in the Middle Ages, though the structure was subject to substantial reconstruction in the 1960s.

Beyond the second installation the route crosses an attractive stretch of pastureland and brings you down to the elegant **double-arched pedestrian bridge** that marks the entrance to the village of **Lavertezzo**. ◀ Once over the bridge head R along the main road for 5 min to reach Lavertezzo's bus stop and eating places.

WALK 19
Revöira and Ca d Dént

Start	Lavertezzo Paese bus stop
Finish	Motta bus stop
Distance	4km (2.5 miles)
Ascent	420m
Descent	340m
Difficulty	Grade 2
Walking time	1 hr 30 min
Terrain	Mainly woodland paths, with some metalled roads and vehicle tracks
Refreshments	There are places serving food and drink in both Lavertezzo and Motta, but neither place has a shop, so stock up on water and snacks in Locarno before boarding the bus.

The steep eastern flanks of the Verzasca valley above Lavertezzo once suffered acutely from water shortages. The unique geology and topography of the area meant that any rainwater that fell in this part of the valley simply ran uselessly off the precipitous slopes or infiltrated the deep substrata of the rocks, to emerge at distant springs. However, on the *maggenghi* of Revöira and Ca d Dént it was discovered that a quirk of geology meant that water circulated all year just below the ground surface (*maggenghi* are upper slopes of a valley where grazing or haymaking takes place in the month of *Maggio*, or May). This led to a system of wells and tanks being established on the valley sides that allowed livestock to graze here in autumn and spring, before and after their time spent the high summer pastures. The preserved ruins of these wells, along with various cisterns, stables, living quarters and other farm buildings, can be seen on a track that follows the ancient transhumance (seasonal animal herding) routes of the Verzasca valley, beginning in Lavertezzo, rising to Revöira, passing through a second cluster of ruins at Ca d Dént and returning to the valley floor once more at Motta. The heritage of the valley is explained in English on a number of information boards. Note that it's easy to combine this walk with Walk 18, which links Motta with Lavertezzo along the valley floor.

ACCESS

Both Lavertezzo and Motta are on the #321 bus route. Some buses run direct from Locarno; otherwise take a train from Locarno to Tenero (5 min journey time) and pick up the bus from there. Buses from Tenero run every 60–90 minutes (less frequently from Locarno). Journey times from Tenero are 29 min (Lavertezzo) and 36 min (Motta).

You can pick up the track marker posts (and read something of the cultural heritage of the area) just by the bus stop in **Lavertezzo**. Revöira and Motta are listed clearly as walking destinations: you begin by heading up the cobbled street by the church and then turning immediately L, following markers that take you along the back lanes of Lavertezzo and then through **Sambugaro**. Sambugaro is a typical carless and picturesque Ticinese village of sturdy stone houses, wandering cats and secretive lanes.

Lavertezzo, the start of the walk

You leave Sambugaro by climbing a final flight of steps and following a path into the chestnut forests, where after a few minutes you arrive at a sign (one of the 'ethnographic route' markers) that gives you the choice of I Maggenghi to the R, or Scandurásc'a, which is a short distance off the path to the L. Scandurásc'a comprises scant remains of a settlement abandoned some two centuries ago, barely visible amidst the boulders of a prehistoric landslide and the encroaching woods. Following the path on through the trees to I Maggenghi will bring you to the first of the three Revöira *magganghi*, named al Mátro, reached 45 min after leaving the bus stop. Invisible from here, though just a short walk up the hillside (signposted), are two further groups of buildings, **Murísc** and immediately above it **ar Cistèrna**, which make for a more appealing (and photogenic) assemblage of ruins.

Between Murísc and ar Cistèrna is a yellow track marker post pointing the way down to Motta. Within 5 min this path runs through the ruins of **Ca d Dént**, the second of the two *maggenghi*, before entering a beech forest. ▶ Just over 30 min of pleasant woodland walking later the path will lead onto the main road right at the **Motta** bus stop.

The **Osteria Motta** (closed Tues) is adjacent to the bus stop. Its outdoor terrace, overlooking the river, is a good place to refresh yourself after this fairly undemanding walk. Some 150m on along the road is a pedestrian foot bridge which will take you to the west bank of the river, where you can walk back to Lavertezzo on the Sentiero per l'Arte (Walk 18).

The beech trees here were planted in the 1940s to stabilize slopes stripped bare over the centuries by deforestation of their natural tree coverage.

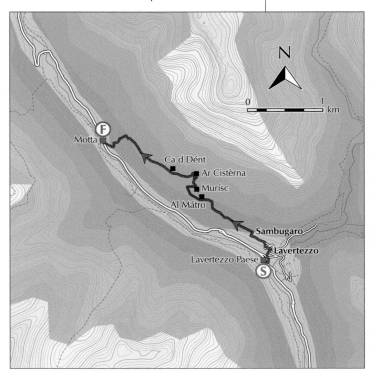

147

WALK 20
Lavertezzo to the Verzasca Dam

Start	Lavertezzo Paese bus stop
Finish	Diga Verzasca bus stop
Distance	11.5km (7 miles)
Ascent	550m
Descent	600m
Difficulty	Grade 2
Walking time	4 hr
Terrain	Well-maintained forest paths; metalled roads at end
Refreshments	Lavertezzo has a number of cafés and restaurants. There is a small shop selling refreshments at the dam.

While the road hugs the eastern side of the chasm-like Verzasca valley, the western side can only be accessed by a well-made footpath (a former mule track) that runs through the forest, affording fantastic views over the river and its dramatic valley, the villages along its banks, and latterly the giant Verzasca Dam and the eastern end of Lake Maggiore. There is some ascending to do as the path crests the bluffs that form the steep valley sides, but the going is generally easy under foot, and the route passes through two attractive hillside villages, Corippo and Mergoscia, as well as giving an opportunity for walkers to admire two very different feats of engineering – the handsome arched medieval bridges at Lavertezzo, and the Verzasca Dam itself. Both Corippo and Mergoscia have bus services to Locarno, making it easy to break the walk into sections or shorten it, and with the walk not straying above the 900m contour this is an ideal poor-weather-day option: there are plenty of opportunities to seek shelter should the weather turn nasty en-route.

ACCESS

Both Lavertezzo and Diga Verzasca are on the #321 bus route. Some buses run direct from Locarno; otherwise take a train from Locarno to Tenero (5 min journey time) and pick up the bus from there. Buses from Tenero run every 60–90 minutes (less frequently from Locarno). Journey times from Tenero are 29 min (Lavertezzo) and 13 min (Diga Verzasca).

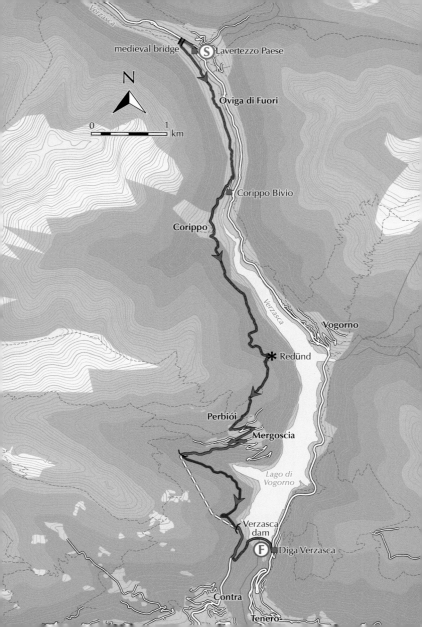

The track marker post opposite the steps up to the church at **Lavertezzo**, just along the road from the bus stop, points the way to Corippo and Tenero. The path drops down to the river then rises again to a parking area before dropping once more to cross the two **medieval arched bridges** (5 min or less from the bus stop). Once the second bridge is crossed turn L across a wooden foot bridge (again signed Corippo) to join a path that clings to the western side of the forested valley, assuming a generally level gradient.

Some 20 min from the bridges you'll pass through a cluster of stone dwellings at **Oviga di Fuori**, 20 min after which there is a torrent to ford. ◄ Some 5 min later you'll pass an impressive weir on the river, after which the path zig-zags up to a hairpin bend on the road running up to Corippo (the road is reached 5 min after the weir).

The torrent is easy to ford but is swollen after rain – in which case you may need to take your shoes and socks off!

> Turning left along this road you'll reach **Corippo Bivio** bus stop (on the #321 route) in just 4 min. There's a sturdy bus shelter to wait at and a traditional Ticino *grotto*, the Corippo Osteria (closed Mon and Tues), which serves basic dishes such as risotto and gnocchetti.

Heading up the road (R) from the hairpin you reach the village of **Corippo** in 10 min. Corippo is an attractive stone-built village but with its permanent population of just nine, it is counted as the smallest municipality in Switzerland. The track marker post opposite the entrance to the church sends you down the hill on flights of steps and then across a torrent on an ancient arched bridge. The path then takes you back into the forest; a R turn up a flight of steps just after the bridge announces the beginning of a steady climb.

Some 45 min after Corippo there's a chance to rest at a purpose-made lookout point over the valley at **Redünd**, after which there's a steep section of zig-zags (mostly steps), levelling off after around 25 min into a marshy valley. After 5 min walking along this valley you reach a collection of buildings at **Perbiói**, which is really the uppermost part of Mergoscia. A track marker post points you down into the village along steep lanes that finally drop you onto a metalled road beside a small chapel. Head down the road around the hairpin bend and drop once again down some steps (L) to reach the main square of **Mergoscia** (20 min after Perbiói).

> There is a fantastic view towards the dam from the benches outside the church that fronts the **main square**. You may find a van selling basic snacks parked up in the square, from where hourly buses run down to Locarno.

From the square pick up the route to Contra, signed on the track marker post. ▶ You need to walk along the road for 20 min, around a series of hairpins, until it disappears into a tunnel, where you can walk along the old road that cars used before the tunnel was built. After 25 min you rejoin the road as it emerges from the tunnel

The section from Mergoscia to the dam is almost wholly along metalled roads.

The view over the Verzasca valley from the walk

– but only for 10 min, as a path is then signed L down into the trees which brings you after another 10 min to the western end of the **Verzasca Dam** (Diga Verzasca). Walk across the dam to its eastern end (5 min) where there is a shop selling refreshments and souvenirs by the bus stop on the main road.

THE VERZASCA DAM

The Verzasca Dam (also known as the Contra Dam or the Locarno Dam) was constructed in the early 1960s; the weight of water behind it, forming Lago di Vogorno, was enough to create a series of minor earthquakes in the years after it was filled. At 220m the dam is awesomely high (and ranks at position 35 in the list of the world's highest dams). In 1995 the opening scenes of the James Bond film *Goldeneye* were filmed here: Bond appears to bungee jump off the dam, purportedly to infiltrate a Russian chemical weapons establishment (the actual jump was performed by a stuntman, and in one poll was voted the best movie stunt of all time). The dam has been a popular centre for bungee jumping ever since, with jumping days always attracting a good throng of spectators.

WALKS FROM
BELLINZONA AND BIASCA

The trail through the Val di Campo (Walk 29)

The trail (top left) above the Val Blenio between Capanna Piandios and Capanna Gorda (Walk 28)

WALKS FROM BELLINZONA AND BIASCA

The towns of Bellinzona and Biasca lie at the geographical heart of Ticino. The former is the cantonal capital, an important business, industrial and commercial hub with an attractive town centre; some 20km to the north (just 17 minutes by train), Biasca is a smaller place that doesn't feature highly on the tourist trail. In terms of their appeal to walkers, the towns have several advantages – they are major public transport hubs, with a wide network of buses fanning out from their stations into the surrounding mountains; their position at the heart of the canton means that all the walks described in this book are actually within striking distance (Lugano and Locarno are both around 20 minutes by train from Bellinzona, while Airolo is 45 minutes by train from Biasca); and being business rather than tourist centres, accommodation is also rather more affordable in these towns than in the lakeside resorts. If you're not that interested in having a sumptuous view from the windows of your accommodation, and you're making considerable use of public transport to get around, then either place makes an ideal centre for walking in Ticino.

BELLINZONA

The three castles that overlook Bellinzona from different heights (and which together are a UNESCO World Heritage Site) are indicative of the town's historical importance as the 'guardian' of routes leading up to the Gotthard Pass. The old town, situated 500m from the station, is focused on the elegant Renaissance buildings that surround the Piazza Collegiata, which is overlooked by the oldest and largest castle, the Castelgrande, inside whose walls are restored walk-through court-yards, a historical museum and a restaurant; the Castello Montebello (90m above the town) and Castello Sasso Cobaro (a further 150m higher) also house museums and provide fine views over Bellinzona and the Ticino valley. There's a fair amount of choice in terms of accommodation spread throughout the town, including the business-oriented Internazionale Hotel opposite the station (hotel-internazionale.ch) and a youth hostel (www.youthhostel.ch/bellinzona), which is housed in a grand cliffside villa a 10–15 minute (level) walk from the station.

The nine walks in the section below that can be accessed by bus from Bellinzona (or a combination of bus and train) mostly explore the wooded slopes of the Ticino valley close by. Sometimes there's a historical focus: Walk 22 passes the ruins of an abandoned village, Walk 23 passes the remains of former iron smelters while Walk 25 looks at the so-called

'hunger towers', built in the nineteenth century to relieve local poverty and strengthen military defences; the other walks head for higher ground, with the wildest scenery encountered in Walk 24, whose destination is a remote *capanna* situated on a rocky ridge some 1600m above the busy activity of the Ticino valley. Walk 26 provides a blend of both scenery and history, rising to another mountain *capanna* and then dropping down to Ticino's largest monastery, while one unusual highlight of the region is the extraordinary Tibetan Bridge (Ponte Tibetano), which spans a gorge above Bellinzona and is the focus of Walk 21. Throughout, the emphasis is on views over the Ticino valley (and sometimes further afield, to Lakes Lugano and Maggiore) with high points accessed via trails that mainly run through thick woodland, though occasionally rise above the treeline into higher scenery.

BIASCA

Biasca unfortunately holds little appeal in itself – its one sight being the Church of San Pietro e Paolo above the town, with its uneven floor hewn from the bedrock and its walls adorned with blood-curdling medieval frescoes – but it gives access to the Val Blenio, one of the most beautiful side valleys in Ticino, a major centre for walking (and in winter for skiing).

The valley's main focus is the small (and unfortunately rather bland) town of Olivone, at the base of the Lukamanier Pass (a road pass that links Canton Ticino with Canton Graubünden) and 40 minutes from Biasca by hourly bus. The three walks that end this chapter have Olivone as their start or end point and allow for a thorough exploration of this valley, following routes along the valley floor, along its flanks (beginning at an altitude of nearly 2000m) and finally along the remote Val di Campo, accessed from the summit of the Lukmanier Pass at its northern end.

In terms of accommodation, the rather plain Hotel della Posta (www. hoteldellaposta.ch) lies across the road from Biasca's railway station, and is handy for all the bus links (though note that the town centre is a 750m walk away). However, staying in Olivone will probably mean better scenery from your hotel room window. A number of possibilities exist here, and along the length of the valley – one distinctive place to check out is the Campra Lodge (www. campralodge.ch), opened in 2019

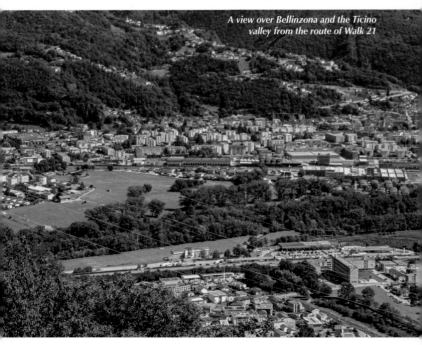

A view over Bellinzona and the Ticino valley from the route of Walk 21

and aimed at winter cross-country skiers and summer hikers, which features contemporary styling throughout, rooms with balconies, a sun terrace and a spa – it's on the road up from Olivone to the Lukmanier Pass and although it's served by a dedicated bus stop, be warned that only four buses pass this way each day in summer.

INFORMATION AND MAPS

Bellinzona's tourist office is in the Palazzo Civico, located 50m southwest of the main Piazza Collegiata (open Mon–Fri 9am–6pm, Sat 9am–4pm and Sun 10am–4pm). Olivone's tourist office is on the main road through the town at Via Lavorceno 1 (open Mon–Fri 8.30am–noon and 1–6pm, Sat and Sun 8am–noon). Biasca's tourist office is in the railway station (open Mon–Fri only, 8.30am–noon and 1–5pm). For maps, use the 1:50,000 Swisstopo maps 266T Valle Leventina for the Val Blenio and 276T Val Verzasca for the walks around Bellinzona. The 1:25,000 Bellinzona Gaborogno Trekking map also covers the walks accessible from Bellinzona, but not the Val Blenio.

PUBLIC TRANSPORT

Trains
Intercity, international and local trains stop at Bellinzona, but only local trains stop at Biasca.

Buses
Buses leave from outside Bellinzona and Biasca stations. In Bellinzona they are the familiar yellow postbuses, but buses serving the Val Olivone are operated by a private company, Autolinee Bleniesi, and have a green and white livery. The main stops are outside Biasca station and at Olivone Posta. At Acquarossa, half way along the valley, there's a large bus interchange – the name of the stop here is Comprovasco.

WALK 21

Monte Carasso, Sementina and the Ponte Tibetano

Start/finish	Monte Carasso Cunvént bus stop
Distance	8.25km (5 miles)
Ascent/descent	760m
Difficulty	Grade 2
Walking time	3 hr 30 min
Terrain	Metalled roads and paved lanes in the first and last part of the walk; woodland paths in the main part
Refreshments	There's a restaurant in Curzútt, and the walk passes a large Co-op supermarket in Sementina (closed Sundays).

This walk starts in Monte Carasso, a southwestern suburb of Bellinzona, and follows the tracks that criss-cross the steep valley sides that rise above it and the neighbouring suburb of Sementina, taking walkers through vineyards and, higher up, through dense forest. The main attraction on the walk is the spectacular Ponte Tibetano pedestrian suspension bridge, opened in 2015, that spans a deep chasm cut into the hillside by the River Sementina. There are also views over the broad Ticino valley to enjoy, along with a fine medieval church with colourful frescoes; the latter is close to the pretty village of Curzútt, a midway stop on the Mornera cable car, whose base station is a couple of minutes' walk from the start of the walk at Cunvént bus stop. The walk, however, assumes that the cable car is not used, which means that there's a good 40 min or so of stiff uphill walking to get under your belt at first; once that's done much of the rest of the walk is undulating or downhill. Paths are well-maintained throughout, navigation is easy, and the forest gives protection from rain and sun. The walk reaches a maximum altitude of only 800m which makes it accessible at most times of the year and in most weathers.

ACCESS

Monte Carasso Cunvént is a stop for both the #311 bus (Bellinzona-Locarno) and the #2 bus (Bellinzona-Giubiasco); buses are frequent (every 15 min Mon–Sat; every 30 min Sun) and journey time from Bellinzona is 7–12 min.

From Cunvént bus stop, follow the main road towards Locarno, crossing the River Sementina after 5 min into the workaday settlement of **Sementina**. Turn R immediately after the bridge (unless you are heading for the Co-op, a few steps further on): the route is marked as the 'Via delle vigne' (Route of the Vines) and moments later a second marker post, under a stone arch, points the way to the village of San Defendente, up a rough flight of steps.

At the top of the steps turn L along a vehicle track. ▶ Beyond the junction the track drops steadily downwards, before the route sends you along a minor road which rises up the hillside. Some 15 min from the junction you pass a road sign pointing the way to

The junction, set amidst vineyards, is overlooked by one of Bellinzona's so-called 'hunger towers' (see Walk 25).

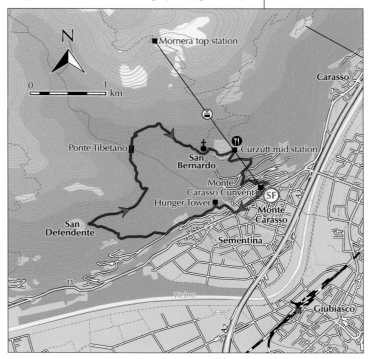

159

The Ponte Tibetano suspension bridge is the highlight of this walk

San Defendente; ignore this but instead take the path which ascends the hillside a few steps further on. From here it's a steady 40 min climb up through the trees to the village; you'll pass a self-service bar with cold drinks (pay via the honesty box) after around 15 min.

> **San Defendente** is a picturesque village but the ancient church is locked and visitors do not seem to be encouraged; its heart is located a minute or so from the track marker post at the top of the climb (turn L and cross the bridge).

From San Defendente pick up the signs for **Ponte Tibetano** that send you back into the forest. The path undulates through the trees, eventually dropping down to the western end of the bridge after 25 min.

> The bridge – known the **Ponte Tibetano Carasc** (Tibetan Bridge) – is, at some 270m long, a spectacular affair, though not recommended for vertigo sufferers. The swaying of the bridge caused by a multitude of feet crossing it is not easily forgotten – and nor is the sight of the deep chasm opening up beneath you: at the centre of the bridge you'll find yourself a heart-stopping 130m above the valley floor.

After crossing the bridge it's an easy 45 min to the medieval church of **San Bernardo**, whose sturdy stone bell tower pokes up through the trees on the valley flanks. ▸ A well-made path links the church with the picturesque village of **Curzútt**, some 10 min further on.

The Romanesque church, which dates from around 1100, is known for its beautifully preserved late-medieval frescoes, and is open Weds–Sun 10am–5pm.

> **Curzútt** is a good place to linger, particularly on a warm afternoon: on fine days it's full of picnicking families who have come up on the cable car from Monte Carasso, and there's also a restaurant, the Ristorante Ostello.

From the village, track signs point the way back down to Monte Carasso via a series of steep paths and flights of stone steps, past shady villas set amidst vineyards and, latterly, between pastel-coloured apartment blocks. ▸ Reckon on 40 min to reach **Monte Carasso** – the route brings you out at the cable car base station, from where it's a few steps to the main road and a R turn to reach the bus stop.

It can be burning hot on these south-facing slopes at the end of a sunny summer's day.

WALK 22

Capanna Genzianella and Motto della Croce

Start/finish	Artore bus stop
Distance	12.75km (8 miles)
Ascent/descent	1190m
Difficulty	Grade 2
Walking time	5 hr 45 min
Terrain	Paved and constructed path to begin with, then woodland paths and vehicle tracks
Refreshments	There's no shop or eating place in Artore. Buy provisions from the supermarket below Bellinzona station before boarding the bus. En route, the Capanna Genzianella offers limited snacks and drinks.

The valley sides that rise to the east of Bellinzona are covered with dense chestnut and silver birch forests whose clearings allow for jaw-dropping views up and down the valley of the Ticino river towards Lake Maggiore. This circular walk runs almost exclusively through these forests, starting in the village-like suburb of Artore, which clings to the flanks of the valley above the heart of Bellinzona, and rising to a height of 1500m – making the route free of snow for much, though certainly not all, of the year. The ascent from Artore is strenuous but what makes this walk worthwhile are three specific stops along the route – namely the Motto della Croce viewpoint, the Capanna Genzianella mountain hut, and the eerily abandoned village of Prada.

ACCESS

Artore bus stop is on route #4 from Bellinzona station (most buses continue on to Castello Sasso Corbaro, the final stop); journey time is 7 min. Buses run every 30–90 min through the day, with services more frequent in the early morning and late afternoon.

Artore bus stop is on a hairpin bend. Start by taking the Via Lobbia, which branches off at the hairpin and runs along the level for 150m into the centre of Artore. Here you'll find the first track marker post, which points the way to Monti di Artore, up a cobbled lane that winds up through the village. Follow the red and white markers up to a road, turn L and after a few steps you'll see markers (easily missed) pointing you R up another lane.

Some 15 min after leaving the bus stop you reach another track marker post, this one giving Motto della Croce – the walk's first stopping point – as a destination. The cobbled path now leads up through a dense chestnut forest, and after 45 min of steady climbing you

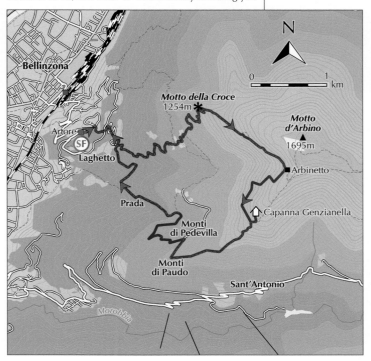

163

The viewpoint Motto della Croce is one of the highlights of this walk

The views from here are breathtaking, stretching to Locarno and Lake Maggiore in one direction, and along the main valley of the Ticino river in the other.

This is the highest point reached on the walk but unfortunately there's no view, because of the thick surrounding of trees.

reach another marker post, situated beside an isolated house, where views begin to open up towards Lake Maggiore. From here it's a little less than an hour's walk up through the trees – the paved path giving way to forest tracks that wind steeply up the hillside – to the distinctive lattice-work cross at **Motto della Croce** (not to be confused with a different viewpoint above Lugano with the same name). ◄

From Motto della Croce take the path marked as leading to Arbinetto. The path again leads into the forest, still rising and – after 20 min – merging with a wider track. Some 15 min later you will reach **Arbinetto**, an isolated house set amidst trees at an altitude of 1494m. ◄ Capanna Genzianella, the next destination to aim for, is signed from here, on a route that takes you down through trees and then, after 5 min, steeply down (R) into the forest. There's not much of a distinct path but the red and white markers painted on trees lead you down and then L, to a three-way track junction (after

20 min) that again signposts the Capanna Genzianella. Within 10 min you emerge from the trees and onto a sunny plateau (the Piano Dolce) that is scattered with an attractive array of isolated houses and buildings – one of which (the uppermost) is the **Capanna Genzianella** (signposted up a steeply rising path).

> The **Capanna Genzianella** (tel 091 857 37 74) is a traditional, basic mountain hut that was converted from a stables in the 1960s. It offers basic snacks and drinks and has dormitory accommodation; when there's no custodian present an honesty box system operates for those who want a beer or soft drink from the fridge. A signboard just below the *capanna* indicates the mountains that can be seen from this vantage point – including, in the far distance, the Monte Rosa massif.

The track marker post below the *capanna* points the way to the hamlet of Monti di Pedevilla. There's no real path through the silver birch forests that cling to the northern flanks of the Morobbia valley, but the red and white marker signs that guide you through the trees are plentiful. After 35 min they bring you out to a picnic area at **Monti di Paudo**. From here Monti de Pedevilla is again signed, the route now heading NE and reaching a road after 10–15 min. Turn L onto the road and then R after 5 min, then watch out for the markers which send you L down a grassy lane after just a few metres. The lane leads you down through the hamlet of **Monti di Pedevilla** onto a metalled road, where you should turn L and then R at the next junction. At the next hairpin bend there's a sign to Prada, sending you once more into the forest.

Following the paths through the forest lead you after 35 min to the ruined buildings in a forest clearing that once formed the village of **Prada**.

> **Prada** had a population of around 120 in the Middle Ages, but declined over the course of the seventeenth and eighteenth century. The village

The walk passes through the abandoned village of Prada, now in ruins

was eventually abandoned and all that remains of it today is a spread of eerily atmospheric ruins. However, in recent years a programme of restoration has been inaugurated; you can read about the history of the village, and the restoration programme, on an information board just below the church.

From Prada you should pick up the signs to Artore that send you right through the heart of the ruins and back, once more, into the forest. In 20 min the path leads you down to a wooden footbridge that spans a rushing torrent. Beyond this the path runs past the houses that form the scattered settlement of **Laghetto**, after which you will find yourself retracing your steps as the route rejoins the cobbled path that marked the start of the walk. Some 45 min after leaving Prada the route leads you into the heart of the village of **Artore**: turn L onto the Via Lobbia to reach the bus stop.

WALK 23

The 'Iron Route' from Carena

Start/finish	Carena bus stop
Distance	14km (8.75 miles)
Ascent/descent	770m
Difficulty	Grade 2
Walking time	5 hr (including diversion to industrial ruins at Maglio di Carena)
Terrain	Metalled roads and vehicle tracks in the first and last part of the walk; woodland paths in the main part
Refreshments	There's no shop in Carena. Stock up on food and water in Giubiasco or Bellinzona. The Ristorante della Posta on Carena's main street (walk 50m west from the bus stop; closed Monday and Tuesday) will be a welcome place to rest up at the end of the walk.

The valley of the tumbling Morobbia river pokes east from Bellinzona's southern extension Giubiasco into the massif that forms the border with Italy. Until the beginning of the eighteenth century this was a centre of iron ore mining and smelting, and ruins of furnaces and a reconstructed charcoal pit can be seen at the start and end of the walk. Between them is a steep ascent through forest to a spectacular eyrie with views down Lake Maggiore to Locarno and the mountains beyond. There's a fair bit of uphill slog in the middle third of the walk, but it's worth it both for the views, and the sense of isolation – few seem to have discovered this quiet valley of thick pine forest and industrial ruins. You'll see the sign 'La Via del Ferro' from time to time along the path – it means 'iron route' and refers, of course, to the mining heritage of the area (and this is in fact only a short section of the path, which extends east across the border).

ACCESS

Bus #212 from outside Giubiasco station (served by local trains running from Bellinzona to Locarno and Lugano) terminates at Carena (hourly or every two hours; 34 min journey time).

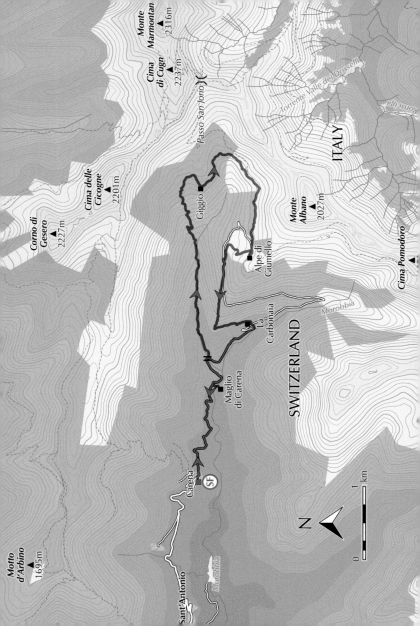

Monte
Marmontan
2316m

Cima
di Cugn
2237m

Torrente Valle dei Dossell

Passo San Iorio

ITALY

Cima delle
Cicogne
2201m

Giggio

Monte
Albano
2027m

Corno di
Gesero
2227m

Alpe di
Giumello

Cima Pomodoro

La
Carbonaia

Morobbia

SWITZERLAND

Maglio
di Carena

SF
Carena

Motto
d'Arbino
1695m

Morobbia

Sant'Antonio

N

0   1
                     km

Head up the road from the bus stop at **Carena** to reach the track marker posts beside the 'Dogana Svizerra' building.

> This is the old **customs house**. Carena once stood at the head of a trade route that ran along the Morobbia valley, over the Passo San Jorio into Italy and down to the shores of Lake Como. Amazingly, goods were still smuggled over this pass until the 1960s – tobacco, salt and coffee crossing to Italy and rice, meats and cheeses coming the other way.

> The first part of the route is along a vehicle track, staying level (or dropping down slightly). After 20 min you reach some information signs (in Italian) overlooking the **Maglio di Carena** (old smelter ruins, also marked on some maps as 'Forni Vecchi'). Just beyond there's a path down to the ruins (under 5 min) through the trees (signed 'al maglio' – which means 'at the mallet').

IRON SMELTING IN THE MOROBBIA VALLEY

Iron was smelted in this region as long ago as the Middle Ages, when the overlord of this part of Ticino was the Duke of Milan. These smelters were destroyed by Swiss troops in the late fifteenth century as they fought their way south from the Gotthard Pass in an effort to extend Swiss territory. It wasn't until 1792 that an enterprising doctor from Bellinzona named Giovanni Bruni decided to revitalize the industry, realizing that this remote valley was a good site for a blast furnace, with its access to wood (for fuel), water and iron ore. Bruni died in 1795 and the complex was passed between owners until a disastrous fire in 1831 forced operations to cease. Visible today are the remains of the large central building housing a blast furnace, along with other buildings that provided storage and living accommodation.

Beyond the path down to the ruins the road is paved as it passes a smattering of villas. After 10 min the road swings R and crosses a bridge over the Morobbia, where there's a track marker post. Take the route signed L to Giggio and start heading up through the trees, to cross after 10 min a wooden bridge over a torrent. The route

Alpe de Giumello, with the path taken by walkers on the left

Giggio is a private residence which at 1677m is the highest point of the walk.

follows the torrent for 35 min before cutting left up through a clearing (the red-and-white markers are clear throughout). After another 45 min of fairly steep uphill climbing the trees thin out to reveal a pastel orange building, **Giggio**. ◀ Head through the grounds of the house to the track marker post, which indicates Alpe de Giumello.

The marker post affords a spectacular **view** down the Morobbia valley to Lake Maggiore, with the flat promontory on which Locarno and Ascona are situated clearly visible; beyond are the mountains around the Simplon Pass and the Italian town of Domodossola. An ideal place to stop for a picnic!

It's easier going now as the path drops down then levels off, bringing you to the modern farm buildings at **Alpe de Giumello** in 50 min. The next marker post is on the north side of the buildings. It points you N, down through trees and meadowland (follow the red and white marker posts) to a road (after 10 min), which you must walk along for 5 min until a path drops R into the trees. After 30 min you'll come out by **La Carbonaia**. ▸ Don't follow the road here – instead, drop down again through the trees for less than 5 min to a lower section of the same road, and then turn L. After 15 min you'll be back at the bridge over the Morobbia, from where you should retrace your steps along the vehicle track to **Carena** (30 min).

This is a mock-up of one of the pits where wood from the nearby forests was heated to produce charcoal, which was then used in the local blast furnaces.

WALK 24

Mornera and the Capanna Albagno

Start/finish	Mornera cable car top station
Distance	6km (3.75 miles)
Ascent/descent	530m
Difficulty	Grade 2
Walking time	2 hr 30 min
Terrain	Forest paths rising to mountain paths around the *capanna*
Refreshments	At the *capanna* and at the café by the cable car top station; there's a grocery store, Quintorno, 70m on along the main road from the I Fracc turn-off (see below; closed noon-3pm and all day Sun).

This great little walk may be short but it ends in high, beguilingly wild countryside and terminates at one of Ticino's most accessible yet remotely-situated *capannas* – all thanks to the Mornera cable car taking most of the strain in terms of altitude-climbing (the walk's Grade 2 rating is down to the central section up through the trees being rather steep). In the final parts there are stunning views all the way to Lake Lugano. This is a fantastic walk for a fine morning or afternoon – or make a day of it and visit the Tibetan Bridge (see Walk 21) from the cable car's midway station. Because of the popularity of the bridge the cable car gets busy and it is strongly advised that you reserve in advance, via their website (www.mornera.ch).

ACCESS

#B2 or #B311 bus from Bellinzona station to Monte Carasso Funivia (up to 4 hourly, journey time 11 min); then walk 140m on along the road and turn R on I Fracc to reach the cable car base station.

From the cable car's top station take the path signed to Alpe de Gariss, heading up into the trees. After 5 min there's a L turn and 10 min later you reach a small lake which you need to keep on your immediate L as you take the path rising still further into the forest. Just a couple of min further on there's a R turning (signed Capanna

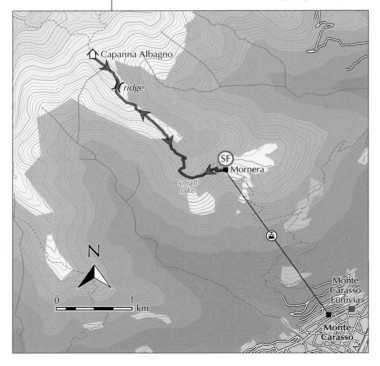

Albagno) which is the start of a steep 20 min climb up through the forest. ▸

At the top of the climb the path levels off and the trees thin out for a more level section along the side of a steep ridge. Things get steeper again after 20 min, with a few zig-zags to crest a ridge separating the Sementina valley from the wilder Gorduno valley. ▸ The countryside becomes rocky and wild for the last 30 min to the **capanna** (which you'll see around 10 min before you reach it) – though most of the climbing has now been done and the path is more level now.

To return, simply retrace your steps back to **Mornera**.

The **Capanna Albagno** (079 274 2250) is a simple two-storey stone building set at an altitude of 1870m and tucked under a ridge that overlooks the Alpe Albagno. To gain a good view over it and the surrounding countryside (and, once again, the curling arms of Lake Lugano) walk a little way N along

The route could be better marked here – keep your eyes peeled for markers on the trees.

There are fantastic views from here over to the curling arms of Lake Lugano.

The Capanna Albagno is situated in wild countryside in the mountains above Bellinzona

the steeply-rising path signed to Alpe di Gariss and Gaggio. The *capanna* serves drinks and simple snacks and there are 28 beds available (book in advance for overnight stays).

WALK 25
Camorino and the Hunger Towers

Start/finish	Camorino Villagio bus stop
Distance	5.25km (3.25 miles)
Ascent/descent	280m
Difficulty	Grade 1
Walking time	1 hr 40 min
Terrain	Forest trails, vehicle tracks and metalled roads
Refreshments	The walk passes the Ristorante Centrale in Camorino (around 60m from the bus stop; closed 2–5pm and all day Mon and Tues).

This relatively easy walk (with a couple of short, steep ascents and descents) investigates some of the remaining 'hunger towers' (*fortini della fame* in Italian) south of Bellinzona whose construction in the nineteenth century deliberately provided work for the local poor. The walk starts in Camorino, essentially a southwestern extension of Bellinzona, and rises into the neighbouring forest, where some of the towers linger amidst the trees. There are views over the Ticino valley but this walk is no show-stopper, scenery-wise; it will, however, be of interest to those wanting to find out more about Ticino's history, while the fact that the walk does not rise above 540m means that it will be accessible for much of the year and in most weathers. Note that this walk is unusual as it does not make use of trail signs, though you will see a number of brown-background tourist signs pointing the way to 'Fortini della fame' along the way.

ACCESS

Bus #B1 runs directly from Bellinzona to Camorino (24 min journey time), or take a train from Bellinzona to Giubiasco (4 min journey time) and then take a bus from outside the station (5 min journey time).

From the bus stop head SE along In Piazza and turn L along a narrow lane, Da Scima, to reach the main road, In Muntagna, for a R turn. Follow this road up and L over the river and around the hairpin to reach (10–15 min from the bus stop) the first tower, **Ai Scarsitt**, where there's a small exhibition about the towers.

Map scale is 1:40,000

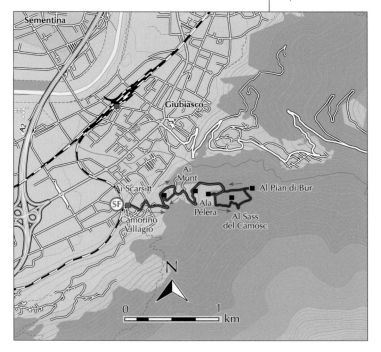

175

One of the so-called hunger towers

Given Switzerland's high living standards today it's difficult to believe that the country was beset by considerable poverty in the nineteenth century. In 1854 Henri Dufour, army general, engineer and topographer, had a series of **round towers** built as part of his defensive line against a potential invasion by Joseph Radetzky's Austrian troops. As a result, 500 unemployed and desperately poor local people were able to earn an income, and the fortifications became known as 'hunger towers'.

Another 10 min up the road is the second tower, **Ai Munt**, and after another 10–15 min there's a parking area R which marks the start of a track (1 min) to the third tower, **Ala Pélera**, which is in ruins. From here head back to the parking area and on along the road. After 100m take the steps that lead L up into the forest. There's a climb now along a well-made forest path that brings you after 5–10 min to the fourth tower, **Al Sass del Camósc**, which is also in ruins.

Leaving the fourth tower, carry on along the track E as it rises up (after 3 min) to a metalled road. Turn L then after 40m take the signed path into the trees. Cross the disused funicular railway and head under the pipeline, then immediately turn L and walk down beside the pipeline to a sign pointing R to the fifth tower, **Al Pian di Bur**, reached 10–15 min after leaving the fourth tower. This tower is also in ruins.

From the last tower, retrace your steps for 50m then drop down to cross the pipeline via a footbridge. The path becomes a vehicle track and crosses the disused funicular tracks before dropping you back onto the metalled road. Turn R here to retrace your steps back down the metalled road to Camorino. After 20 min a left turn on cobbled **Ai Scarsitt** cuts off one of the hairpins on the road – turn L at the T junction at its end to arrive at the bus stop 10 min later.

WALK 26

*Capanna Brogoldone and the
Santa Maria Monastery*

Start	Top station of the Monti-Savorù cable car
Finish	Claro Paese Bus Stop
Distance	10.75km (6.75 miles)
Ascent	650m
Descent	1660m
Difficulty	Grade 2
Walking time	5 hr
Terrain	Woodland paths; cobbled lanes in the last part
Refreshments	There is a Denner supermarket in Lumino (see below), a few steps on along the main road from the bus stop (closed noon–1.30pm and all day Sun). On the walk, the Capanna Brogoldone serves basic drinks and snacks. The walk ends by a Co-op supermarket (closed Sun).

The cable car up Monti-Savorù may be one of Ticino's lesser-known but it whisks you up to a sun-drenched south-facing ledge with great views, from where woodland paths take you first to a look-out over Bellinzona and the Ticino valley, and then up to high pastureland and the Capanna Brogoldone, a mountain hut perched on a ridge that offers basic snacks (and accommodation too if need be). Then it's back down through the woods to the beautiful Santa Maria monastery, which overlooks the valley town of Claro. The ascent through the trees up to the *capanna* is a reasonably tough one but the rewards of the walk – in the form of the spectacular situation of both the *capanna* and the monastery – more than make up for this. This is also a quiet part of the centre of the canton and you are likely to have most of the woodland paths to yourself.

ACCESS

To reach the start of the walk take Bus #B214 from outside Castione-Arbedo station (a stop for local trains between Bellinzona and Biasca) to Lumino Paese (every 30 min; 3 min journey time), from where it's a 400m walk up through the village of Lumino to the Monti-Savorù cable car base station; from Claro Paese the #B8 bus runs to Castione-Arbedo station (every 1–2 hours; 7 min journey time), though a 10-min walk from Claro Paese along Alla Stazione will take you down to Claro Ponton bus stop on the main road, from where services to Castione are more frequent (on the #B221 service). (Despite the name of the road there's no train station here.)

From the top station of the cable car first head SW to Prusciana (signposted). The path runs immediately below the house to the SW of the cable car station, soon after which, just after the path enters the trees, you have to fork R. A level walk along well-made woodland paths will bring you after 10 min to **Prusciana**, a clearing in the trees where there's a smattering of buildings. ◄

From here there's a fabulous view over the meeting point of the Ticino and Moesa valleys and the town of Bellinzona.

Retrace your steps to the cable car top station and take the steps up to the track marker post which points the way to Capanna Brogoldone. After 15 min a sign points out two ways up to the *capanna* – taking the R fork

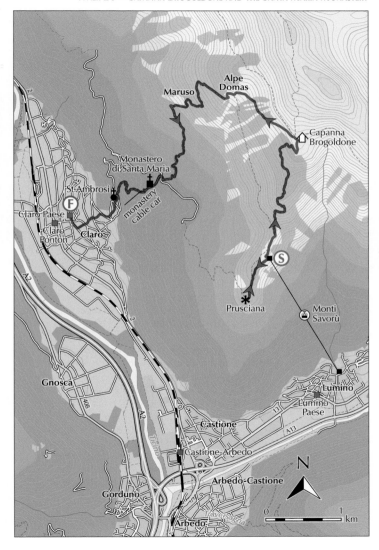

The Capanna Brogoldone offers refreshments in the first part of the walk

here (signposted scorciatoia rapido) takes you on a steady uphill climb of 1 hr 30 min to reach open pastures and the **Capanna Brogoldone**.

The buildings of the **Capanna Brogoldone** (091 829 4350; www.brogoldone.ch) stretch along a high ridge at an altitude of 1903m – the highest point on the walk. There's been a hut for walkers here since 1938, but the place was fully renovated in 1998, with separate buildings for eating and sleeping. In terms of the former there are homemade cakes, local cheeses, and basic but traditional dishes on offer, all to be enjoyed to the accompaniment of predictably fine views. The custodian can give advice and lend equipment for bouldering on the rocky outcrops that surround the hut.

The next track marker post is situated just NW of the hut. Take the path signed Alpe Domas and Maruso, which takes you back into the trees, and after 35 min you reach **Alpe Domas**, which is nothing more than a patch of meadowland and a small farm building. From here the path to the monastery is signed, taking you first to **Maruso** (which also appears as Marùs on some maps and signs; 35 min), a cluster of holiday homes with a splendid view over the valley, and then down to a small parking area (reached after another 15 min).

Cross the parking area and take the flight of steps that drop down once again into the trees. You'll get your first view of the monastery before you reach a road (50 min from the parking area) from where you should walk a few metres along the tarmac before turning L along the sign-posted road that leads to the monastery. After just a couple of minutes there's a track marker post, signing the way to Claro; the entrance to the **Monastero di Santa Maria** is just a few steps along this footpath.

The **monastery** (www.monasterodiclaro.ch) is a working community of eleven Benedictine nuns. Its whitewashed cluster of buildings overlook the village of Claro from a rocky spur, and it was founded

The Monastero di Santa Maria at Claro, which the walk passes in its final stage

in the year 1490, making it the oldest monastery in Ticino. The complex underwent major restoration between 1998 and 2005 and the buildings now form a harmonious whole on the valley sides, set amidst chestnut forests. The chapel can be visited (though the rest of the monastery is private) and you can also buy jams and honey produced by the nuns.

The path down to Claro that passes the monastery's entrance becomes cobbled – not easy on the feet after a day's walking – and takes you past a couple of small chapels and through a narrow defile in the hillside to the **Chapel of St Ambrosi**, reached after 15 min. ◄ Across the road from the chapel signs point the way along more cobbled lanes to the centre of **Claro** (reached after another 15 min) – the signage here is not always clear but you should be aiming for the church, whose tower rises above what is largely a modern settlement. Immediately behind and below the church is a Co-op supermarket; **Claro Paese** bus stop is across the road, outside the curvy whitewashed school building.

Taking the monastery's own cable car will save you this 15-min walk: from the base station head down the road and turn R to reach the St Ambrosi chapel.

WALK 27
Val Blenio Sentiero Storico

Start	Olivone Posta bus stop
Finish	Malvaglia Rongie bus stop
Distance	19km (11.75 miles)
Ascent	190m
Descent	700m
Difficulty	Grade 2
Walking time	4 hr 30 min
Terrain	Mainly easy footpaths through woodland and pastureland; in the southern section metalled roads and vehicle tracks predominate
Refreshments	You can find grocery stores and eating places in the villages this walk passes through.

The Sentiero Storico – literally, 'route of stories' – is a marked and designated route that runs the entire length of the beautiful Val Blenio, taking in some pleasant valley-bottom scenery, traditional villages, fine churches and a ruined castle along the way. Navigation is easy – in fact there are so many waymarker signs that it would be possible to do the walk without a map – and with the path sticking close to the road, along which runs a good bus service, it would be very easy just to do a short section of the route. Sign boards at regular intervals reveal individual stories about the buildings, people and landscape associated with each place along the valley, though unfortunately information is presented only in Italian, German and French. Note that for most of its length the Sentiero Storico follows the route of the Sentiero Bassa – literally the 'lower route' – and on most signs and marker posts you'll see both names (though sometimes only one). South of Acquarossa both routes are a thread of different paths, rather than a single route, though options (in the form of 'via' and intermediate places listed) are always made clear.

ACCESS

Both bus stops are on the #131 bus route from Biasca station to Olivone (hourly).

The information boards along the length of the Sentiero are sponsored by Raiffeisen Bank – and their branch in Olivone (situated right by the main bus stop and the tourist office) marks the official start of the trail.

Start by following the route along the main road back towards **Olivone**. Turning sharp left by the Casa Communale you'll see one of the grandiose, gated villas for which Olivone is known. ▶ A few minutes after passing the Casa Communale the trail takes you past the small Museo Cà da Rivöi, opposite which is the local parish church.

The **Museo Cà da Rivöi** (open by appointment only; phone 091 871 1977) is situated in a fifteenth-century dwelling and consists of ethnographic exhibits (agricultural tools, religious objects and the like)

Many of Olivone's gated villas were built by Milanese chocolate entrepreneurs at the turn of the twentieth century – and other locations in the valley have historical links with chocolate manufacture.

183

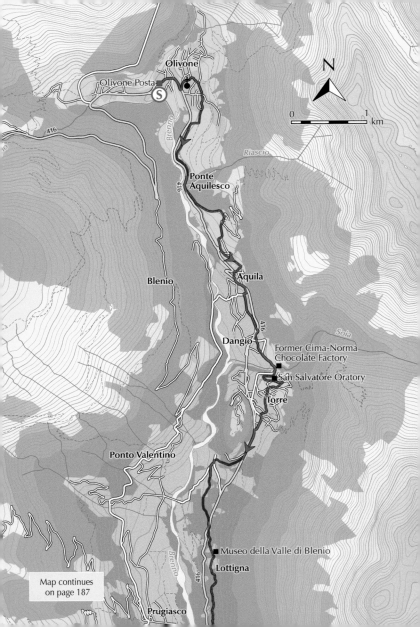

Olivone

Olivone Posta

(S)

Brenno

416

Ponte
Aquilesco

Riascio

Áquila

Blenio

416

Sóia

Dangio

Former Cima-Norma
Chocolate Factory

San Salvatore Oratory

Torre

Ponto Valentino

Brenno

416

Museo della Valle di Blenio

Lottigna

Map continues
on page 187

Prugiasco

from the local area; the parish church is a Baroque building whose square, pyramid-topped tower (dating from 1100) is typical of the Blenio valley.

Beyond the church and the museum, the route winds its way through residential districts of Olivone before taking you out into open countryside and the quiet villages of **Ponte Aquilesco** and then **Aquila**. Around 1 hr 25 min from Olivone you arrive at a slightly larger village, **Dangio**. ▸ Some 5 min beyond the church the trail climbs up beside the monolithic façade of the **former Cima-Norma chocolate factory**.

The **chocolate factory** was founded in 1903 by the Cima brothers from Nice, who were bought out ten years later by another industrialist, Guiseppe Pagani, who owned the Norma chocolate factory in Zurich. At its height the factory employed 300 people, but it closed in 1968; the building is now an exhibition venue and is only open sporadically.

Beyond the old factory building the path rounds a wooded bluff and 10 min later passes the San Salvatore oratory, a medieval foundation whose buildings date from Baroque times. The patch of greenery outside serves as an exhibition space for modern sculpture, but if you're not tempted to linger then the next diversion comes in the form of the **Museo della Valle di Blenio** in **Lottigna** in another 50 min – the trail passes right by the front door.

The **Museo della Valle di Blenio** (open 2–5.30pm, Tue–Sun, Easter–Oct) is housed in a handsome sixteenth-century frescoed villa in the heart of the village; its displays are mainly folkloric and ethnographic items from the local area – costumes, religious objects, paintings and the like.

Around 25 min beyond the museum the trail drops down through thick woodland and deposits you on the main road just outside **Acquarossa**. ▸ If you do not wish

The parish church in Dangio is adorned with a distinctive mural of St Christopher, the patron saint of travellers.

This is the valley's principal town; unfortunately its bland, workaday centre, reached by crossing the bridge over the river here, lacks the charm of the valley's smaller settlements.

The Blenio Valley near Acquarossa

The church dates from 1249 and there are valuable medieval frescoes inside. You need to contact the custodian for the key. Phone details are on the information board.

to enter the town keep on the E bank of the river, following directions on the track marker post to Dongio along the Sentiero Bassa.

At first you will be on a metalled road, the Via Satro, but after 5 min this becomes a track. The track is the **Vecchia Strada del Strato**, an old packhorse trail dating from the early nineteenth century, which hugs the course of the river and makes for easy graded walking. After 10 min you reach the northern outskirts of **Dongio** where you should turn R over the pedestrian **box girder bridge** and then head through the houses on the Via Boscero to reach a track marker post (5 min from the bridge), which sends you L to Ludiano and San Remigio along the metalled Via San Remigio.

After 5 min you pass **San Remigio Church**. ◀ Beyond the church the metalled road swings left, sending you straight on along a vehicle track that heads into the trees.

Cima di
Gana Bianc
2842m ▲

Museo della Valle di Blenio
Lottigna

Prugiasco

Acquarossa
Comprovasco

Acquarossa

Brenno

416

Vecchia Strada del Strato

416

box girder bridge

San Remigio

Dongio

Oratorio di Santa Maria del Monastero

Brenno

416

Sentida →

Cima
Gana Ro

N

0   1
━━━━━━━━ km

Ludiano
Ganna

Serravalle Castle

Semione

F

Malvaglia Rongie
Malvaglia

416

After a minute you need to fork R up a slight rise. Some 15 min later you pass the **Oratorio di Santa Maria del Monastero** (L). This church also has valuable frescoes – but they are later, from the sixteenth to the nineteenth centuries. The same access arrangements apply as for the earlier church. The route now runs through a wooded section with a slightly trickier path, before you come out onto a metalled road at **Sentida**, 25 min beyond the second church.

From the track marker post at Sentida walk along the road as it passes through the quiet village of **Ludiano**. You'll pass the Ludiano Piazza Fiera bus stop after 10 min and then just a couple of min later you need to turn L on the Via Ganne di Fuori, a narrow metalled lane, which drops down through vineyards to a track marker post at **Ganna** (reached after less than 5 min from the turn). This sends you along the road for 40m then R onto a track that curls around more vineyards before bringing you to the northern end of the ruins of **Serravalle Castle** (just over 5 min from Ganna).

To complete the walk, head down from the castle past the chapel and the modern farm buildings to the minor road. Turn L and follow the road as it runs NE then crosses the river to the main road. Ahead is Rongie, the

Serravalle Castle

SERRAVALLE CASTLE

The picturesque ruins of Serravalle Castle, which the walk passes through in its final stage

The castle (24-hour access; no entry charge) dates from the time that this valley was an important routeway that controlled access to the Lukmanier Pass. One of the first mentions of the castle came in 1224, when the Emperor Frederick Barbarossa stayed here for four days when he was leading an army into Italy. The following decade the Milanese, who were overlords of Leventina (the area around Bellinzona) at the time, built a new castle – the one whose ruins can be seen today. The castle was destroyed in 1402 when the Milanese were overrun by an army led by the Graubünden warlord Alberto de Sacco, after which Leventina fell into Graubünden hands.

northern extension of the town of Malvaglia. Cross a parking area to reach an attractive square overlooked by a church. From here Via Ronge takes you through the settlement; turn R at the Ristorante della Posta (closed Weds) along Viale Stazione to reach **Malvaglia Rongie** bus stop (15 min from the castle).

WALK 28
Val Blenio Strada Alta

Start	Top station of Leontica-Cancorì-Pian Nara chairlift
Finish	Olivone Posta bus stop
Distance	13.75km (8.5 miles)
Ascent	280m
Descent	1330m
Difficulty	Grade 2
Walking time	4 hr
Terrain	Well-graded mountain paths, forest trails, vehicle tracks and metalled roads
Refreshments	At Cancorì (middle station of chairlift); en route, at the Capanna Piandios, the Capanna Gordo and the Ospizio Camperio; there are a number of cafes, restaurants and supermarkets around the bus stop in Olivone.

This walk along the Val Blenio's *strada alta*, or upper path, is the best way of appreciating the magnificence of the valley's scenery – and with the chairlift at Leontica taking care of the initial ascent the walk is a comparatively accessible one, with well-graded paths, no steep ascents, and refreshments available at well-placed intervals along the route, most of which is downhill. Starting in high pastureland amidst the ski slopes of Pian Nara, the route gradually drops down into woods and cow-grazed meadowland with dramatic views across the valley to Adula, Ticino's highest peak, before the final approach to Olivone along a narrow river valley. Throughout, the views up and down the valley are stunning – though choose a clear day as the first part of the walk is high and exposed.

ACCESS

Bus #B131 from Biasca to Acquarossa Comprovasco (hourly; journey time 19 min) then Bus #B133 to Leontica Chiesa (every two hours; 15 min journey time), then a 10-min walk to chairlift base station. The chairlift has limited operating hours and days, even in midsummer – check times in advance. At the end of the walk, bus #B131 runs hourly from Olivone Posta to Biasca (journey time 52 min).

The track marker post by the chairlift station at **Pian Nara** (1935m) signposts the way to Capanna Piandios and Olivone along a track that drops down the valley side for a little way, before taking you L under a ski tow and to the R of the buildings at **Cambra**. Head NE from here along a vehicle track that runs along the valley sides at around the 1920m contour, passing the buildings at **Pian Laghetto** (L) after 15 min and then reaching the **Capanna Piandios** 15 min later. ▶ The track marker post on the slope above the hut points out the route across pasture-land to Gorda and Olivone.

The capanna is a small, traditional mountain hut situated at an altitude of 1875m amidst high pastures, offering accommodation and basic drinks and refreshments, with a terrace overlooking the valley.

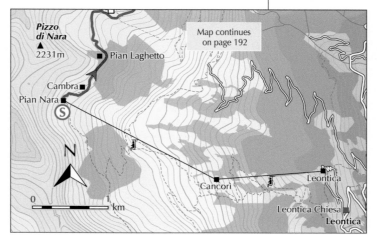

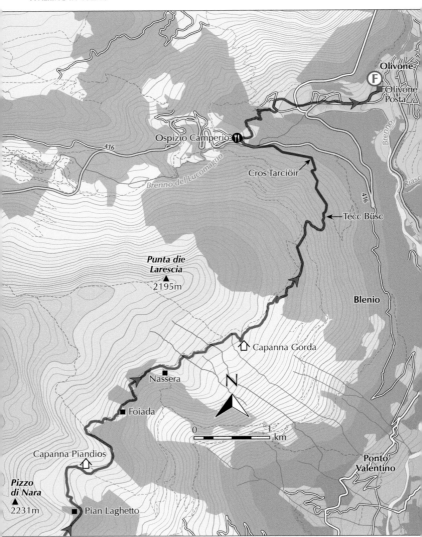

Olivone

F

Olivone
Posta

Ospizio Camperio

Cros Tarciöir

416

Brenno del Lucomagno

Tecc Büsc

Brenno

*Punta die
Larescia*
▲
2195m

Blenio

Capanna Gorda

N

Nassera

Foiada

Capanna Piandios

0   1
km

*Pizzo
di Nara*
▲
2231m

Pian Laghetto

Ponto
Valentino

Follow the route marked out by poles. There's a steady climb now, the only one on the walk, rising just under 100m over 15 min. At the top of the rise a track marker post points you downwards (again to Olivone and Gorda) along a path that runs NE, undulating above and below the treeline, passing clutches of buildings at **Foiada** (35 min from the *capanna*) and then **Nassera** (another 20 min further on) before reaching a spread of farm buildings and holiday homes at Gòrda di Sopra after another 25 min.

> The **Capanna Gorda** (1800m) occupies a wooden chalet to the immediate south of the other buildings at Gòrda di Sopra and offers accommodation and basic refreshments. There's a superb view from the terrace over to the icy peaks of the Adula (better known by its German name, Rheinwaldhorn; 3402m) and the Pizzo di Cassimoi (3128m), the highest parts of a formidable wall of permanently snow-capped mountains that divide Ticino from the neighbouring canton, Graubünden.

The route from the *capanna* drops down through the cluster of buildings to a road, which you should follow for 15 min until a track marker post at a hairpin sends you off the road (N) and onto forest paths and tracks that soon begin to zig-zag down the hillside, before you reach a track marker post by some houses at **Tecc Büsc** (50 min from the *capanna*). Here you are sent L (N) along a minor road. Follow this for a minute before, at a hairpin, you rejoin the network of forest paths, heading N through trees and across meadowland to the track marker post at **Cros Tarciöir**, reached some 15–20 min later. After another 10–15 min you reach the busy road up to the Lukmanier Pass.

Turn L along the road as it spans the Brenno del Lucomagno river. After just 2 min cross the road to pick up the track marker post beside the **Ospizio Camperio**, signing Olivone.

View over the Blenio valley from the trail

The **Ospizio** (closed Mon) offers a range of meals, snacks and drinks and is a favourite with the bikers who are heading for Olivone after roaring their way over the Lukmanier Pass. There's a bus stop on the road here, for buses down to Olivone, though they are not very frequent.

The route now heads along a track and then zig-zags down through the trees to the churning Ri di Piera river. Some 15 min after the Ospizio you join a metalled road, after which the route leads down through **Olivone** along a well-signed series of metalled roads, paths and back lanes. The route finally joins the main road a few minutes before it passes the bus stop outside the Post Office in the town's centre (40 min from the Ospizio).

WALK 29
Lukmanier Pass to Olivone via Passo di Gana Negra

Start	Lukmanier Passhöhe bus stop
Finish	Olivone Posta bus stop
Distance	17km (10.5 miles)
Ascent	520m
Descent	1540m
Difficulty	Grade 3
Walking time	5 hr 30 min
Terrain	Well-graded mountain paths, forest trails, vehicle tracks and metalled roads
Refreshments	At the restaurant at the Lukmanier Passhöhe bus stop; en route, at the Capanna Bovarina and the Ristorante Genziana just outside Campo Blenio; there are shops and cafes around the bus stop in Olivone.

There's a fantastic variety of scenery on this walk, from the high mountain environment of the Passo di Gana Negra to the woods of the lower Val di Campo – and in the final stage comes one of Ticino's most dramatic gorges, cut into the mountainside above Olivone by the Brenno della Greina river. There's a stiff ascent at the beginning as you rise 500m to the summit of the Passo di Gana Negra, but the mountain paths around the summit of the pass are comparatively well-made and well-graded for this altitude (2400m) and after that it's mostly downhill. It's a lengthy walk, though there's an opportunity to cut out the last 45 min down to Olivone, and the rustic Capanna Bovarina makes for a great place to rest up around two-thirds of the way through. Choose a fine day as the first part of the walk is rather exposed (and be warned that it can be chilly and windy on both the Lukmanier and Gana Negra passes).

ACCESS
Hourly buses run from Biasca to Olivone Posta (journey time 40 min) from where there are four daily buses in summer to Lukmanier Passhöhe (journey time 28 min).

The track marker post beside the Hospezi and bus stop at the summit of the Lukmanier Pass points the way to Campo Blenio and the Capanna Bovarina.

The 1917m high pass (**Passo del Lucomagno** in Italian, though it's known more by its German name, Lukmanier Pass) is set amidst some very bleak and unforgiving scenery. The Hospezi Santa Maria (www.lukmanierpass.ch) at the summit provides basic meals, snacks and accommodation. The pass links Canton Ticino with a part of Canton Graubünden where Romansh is spoken – indeed this is the language used in the Hospezi, and the neighbouring lake is called the Lai da Sontga Maria, an unmistakably Romansh name. As you begin the walk you pass a stone plinth announcing that the road over the pass is entering 'Grischun' – the Romansh name for Graubünden.

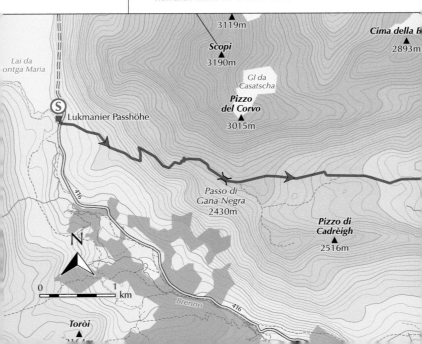

The first stage of the walk rises gently over meadow-land, but the ascent of the pass begins properly after 15 min, with a major zig-zag up the hill followed by a series of minor zig-zags lifting you into the rocky environs of the pass. Around an hour after leaving the bus stop the crest becomes visible and the gradient levels off, and 15 min later (1 hr 15 min from the bus stop) the track marker post at the summit of the **Passo di Gana Negra** (2430m) is reached.

There's a level area at the pass summit to cross before the Val di Campo opens up in front of you. ▷ There's now a lengthy drop down through a dramatic landscape of massive boulders and along the base of the Val di Campo, where the path (clearly marked by red-and-white markers and poles) brings you after 1 hr from the pass summit to the farm buildings at **Alpe di Bovarina**.

Now take the vehicle track that runs along the valley's southern flank. After 5 min a sign to the Capanna Bovarina sends you L along another vehicle track that

Clearly visible in the distance is the Luzzone Dam above Campo Blenio, built in the 1960s. The TV show *Top Gear* once staged a bungee jump from the dam in an occupied car!

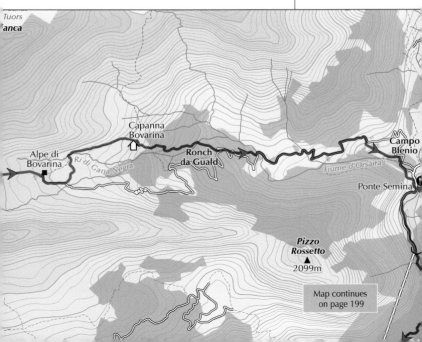

Map continues on page 199

curls round to cross the Ri di Gana Negra stream. Around 300m beyond the bridge a track marker post sends you E across meadowland, and you reach the **Capanna Bovarina** around 10–15 min after that (30 min walking time from Alpe di Bovarina). The *capanna* occupies a cluster of wonderfully traditional buildings. From its terrace there's a view over to the range of 3000m high peaks that mark Ticino's border with Graubünden.

From the *capanna* take the path leading down into the trees signed Campo Blenio. There's 30 min of steep descent until the path crosses the Ri di Gana Negra by a high wooden bridge (25 min from the *capanna*) and becomes a wider track as is passes through a cluster of traditional buildings at **Ronch da Guald** 5 min later. From here for the next 10 min the path crosses and re-crosses a metalled road as both run down the hillside, before walkers have to walk down the road itself for 30 min. Just before the road enters Campo Blenio you are signed R, and the last 10 min into **Campo Blenio** (reached 1 hr 25 min from the *capanna*) is once again on paths.

The Ri di Gana Negra stream

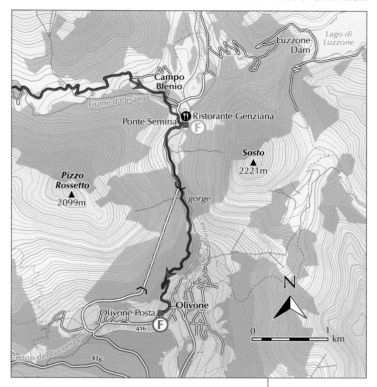

From the parking area at the centre of Campo Blenio (unfortunately rather a bland place) pick up the sign to Olivone, crossing the Fiume d'Orsàira river and then turning R onto a path that runs high above the road. Some 10 min from the parking area you reach the main Olivone to Campo road at the **Ristorante Genziana**. ▶

The first part of the walk from here down to Olivone is unfortunately along the road, but after 5–10 min you can use a path that runs right next to it, before rejoining the road for 200m until it enters a tunnel (around 15 min from the restaurant). Here walkers are sent onto a

Not only is the restaurant a possible refreshment stop, you can end the walk here – there's a bus stop right by it (Ponte Semina) for buses down to Olivone.

The Capanna Bovarina, with the Luzzone Dam in the background

track cut into the cliffside that runs high above a spectacular gorge cut by the Brenno della Greina river. After passing through the gorge the track drops you into the back streets of **Olivone** (30 min from the start of the track at the tunnel mouth). Follow them down onto the main road through Olivone. When you reach it, turn R for the bus stop, just a few metres away (reached in 1hr from the parking area at Campo Blenio).

WALKS FROM AIROLO

Ossasco, one of the villages on Walk 32

The Gotthard Pass: the start of Walks 30 and 31

WALKS FROM AIROLO

On both sides [of the St Gotthard Pass] there are places of terrible
grandeur, unsurpassable, I should imagine, in the world...
Oh God! what a beautiful country it is!

*Charles Dickens in a letter to his future biographer John Forster,
after crossing the St Gotthard Pass in 1846*

Keep on ascending till you reach the height
Of Gotthard, where the everlasting lakes,
Filled by the streams of Heaven, are situated.

Friedrich Schiller, Wilhelm Tell

Here, is really the end of the world. The Gotthard is truly nature's ossuary.
Instead of the bones of the dead lie monstrous rows of bleak rocky mountains...

*German writer Wilhelm Heinse in a letter to his friend and patron
Ludwig Gleim, September 1780*

The Passo del San Gottardo – known to English speakers as the St Gotthard Pass or simply the 'Gotthard' – is one of the most iconic of all Alpine passes. A natural gap in the wall of mountains that separate Ticino from the rest of Switzerland, it has been a trade artery since earliest times, providing a route across the heart of the Alps from Zurich (and Germany beyond) to Milan and Italy.

In former times, traversing the Gotthard was a treacherous affair: even if the weather was kind, the path was steep and devils were rumoured to live among the peaks that glowered over it. The earliest record of a hospice for travellers at the summit of the pass dates from 1237, when the road up and over the pass was a simple mule track. Nowadays a brilliantly-engineered road twists its way from the town of Airolo to the summit of the pass, where a myriad of restaurants and shops ensure that on fine days in summer the place is something of a tourist merry-go-round. Although the road is not cleared of snow in winter, the Zurich–Milan motorway and rail lines burrow through long tunnels a thousand metres below it, ensuring that the Gotthard provides a vital route between northern Europe and Italy that is open year-round.

Whilst traders and travellers have always been able to traverse the Gotthard, the range of mountains through which it passes have proved to be a formidable cultural barrier. The most obvious manifestations of this are actually linguistic rather than political: to the south of this great chain of peaks the principal language is Italian, but to the northwest (in Canton Valais), north (in Canton Uri) and northeast (in Canton Graubünden) it is German and Romansh that hold sway – the latter being Switzerland's fourth language, a distant descendent of Latin.

As far as visitors and walkers are concerned, it is around the southern approaches to the Gotthard – centred around the small town of Airolo – that you'll find some of the most scenically rewarding walks in the Canton. Whilst some of the walking routes thread their way along the sides or bottoms of the deep glacial valleys, other routes head up from these valleys and into the high countryside that towers over them – and the area is dotted with mountain huts for those walkers who are determined to head for the really high ground.

The countryside tends to be dramatic and wild – sometimes bleakly so – forming a contrast to the area further south, where the lakes create an environment that is immediately easier on the eye. But that's just the point: walkers here get to experience the Alps at their most raw, and as far as scenery goes the emphasis is on deep chasms, inaccessible peaks and rocky ridges rather than the 'chocolate box' Switzerland of chalets and cowbells. It must be said, too, that Northwestern Ticino attracts a different type of visitor to the south: the crowds thin out here, and with no lakeside resorts to shop or lounge in and no boat trips to take, the emphasis is firmly on hiking rather than less adventurous holiday making – but the region is none the poorer for that, and with fewer visitors come slightly lower prices in restaurants and hotels, too.

AIROLO

The small town of Airolo is the principal centre of northwestern Ticino and a major hub for public transport. Trains heading north enter the 15km (9.3 miles) Gotthard rail tunnel here, and all trains stop at Airolo's busy station, which is the town's focal point for visitors. Across the road from it, amidst a string of cafes and restaurants, are a bank and a well-stocked supermarket, along with a couple of hotels, the modern, upmarket Forni (Tel 091 869 12 70; www.forni.ch) and the more venerable Hotel des Alpes (Tel 091 869 17 22; www.hotel-desalpes-airolo.ch/) whose somewhat plainer rooms (some of which are not en-suite) come at a rather more affordable price. Falling midway between these in terms of price and facilities is the Hotel Garni BB Motta (Tel 091 869 22 11; www.bbmotta.ch/), situated 100m up the hill from the station on Via San Gottardo, the town's main street.

Airolo makes a great base for walkers (and in winter there's some low-key skiing here, too), but it's a modern, workaday place without any specific historic centre or attractions, and those with a car may wish to stay somewhere more classically Swiss – any number of villages in the surrounding mountains would fit the bill. For public transport users, however, it's unbeatable, and even if the most remarkable feature of the town is (unfortunately) the unsightly coil of elevated roads associated with the southern portal of the Gotthard road tunnel, excursions into the surrounding countryside provide more than adequate compensation. And of course, you don't actually need to stay here to walk in these high mountains, as Airolo is easily reachable on day trips from the lakeside resorts in the south of Ticino: direct trains from Lugano take 90 minutes to reach Airolo while those from Bellinzona take just under an hour.

WALKS FROM AIROLO

Airolo lies at a nexus of routes that thread away from the town in three different directions – and all of which give access to fine walking territory (buses, all of them run by the local postbus service, leave from right outside the station).

Heading north by car or bus you'll be at the top of the Gotthard Pass in an easy 25 minutes, and although it's not a place to hang around, the summit does provide an easily-accessible starting point for some high-altitude walking routes: the first two walks described in this section begin here.

ST GOTTHARD PASS

The Passo del San Gottardo – usually known by its German name, the St Gotthard Pass – is one of the great Alpine passes (www.passosangottardo. ch). Unfortunately, the spread of buildings at the summit is rather ungainly; alongside some ex-military facilities there are a couple of bar/restaurants, a gift shop, and a museum of the Pass (open June–Sept 9am–6pm daily; 14 Fr) – all thronged with visitors at busy times in summer (particularly with the ubiquitous motorcyclists, who love giving their powerful machines a spin over passes such as these). One building that is worth seeking out is the chapel, whose altar is made from stone hewn out of the mountain when the road tunnel was built in the 1970s. However, most walkers will probably want little more than a quick look round at the top before heading on their way. The bus stops right outside the museum and gift shop, with a track marker post just beside the lake and the striking Guex monument. The latter takes the form of a stone cairn on which eagles have apparently perched, waiting to take flight, and is a 1928 work by Fausto Agnelli that commemorates the Swiss aviator Adrien Guex, who died when his plane crashed on the Pass during a reconnaissance flight on 7 August 1927.

The Guex Monument at the Gotthard Pass

The track marker post beside the Guex monument (see box) marks Ronco as being 3 hr 45 min away. From the marker post take the cobbled road (the 'Old Gotthard road') that leads down between the Albergo San Gottardo and the museum/gift shop complex. After just a couple of minutes follow the signs that point you off to the R along a track that leads over a small bridge. Five minutes later, as the track approaches the main road, look for the path that leads left and up (red and white markings) taking you to the right of the electricity pylon but below its wires. After running above the main road for a few minutes the path drops down below it, hugging the base of concrete piers that carry the road. ◄

After 15 min the track rises above the road (eventually crossing over it when it's in a tunnel) and there's a brief climb up to a mule track, which runs spectacularly along the valley side, with views down to Airolo and up to the Gotthard Pass summit. Some 20 min later, beside an isolated but apparently unnamed cluster of buildings,

A few spectacular cascades pour down the cliff edge right beside the path here, but their outflows are no problem to ford.

The old road up the Gotthard Pass as viewed from the walk

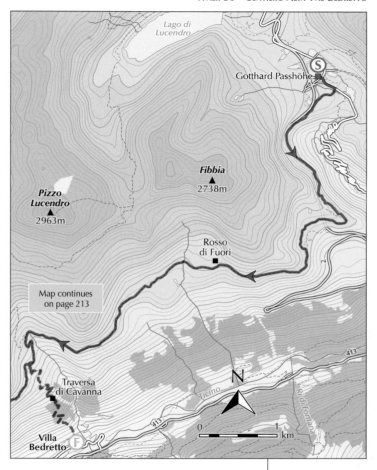

the path becomes a vehicle track and is signposted Sentiero Alto Val Bedretto.

From now on the route follows this vehicle track through high, bleak, exposed countryside, climbing gently to **Rosso di Fuori** (reached after 30 min), a group of

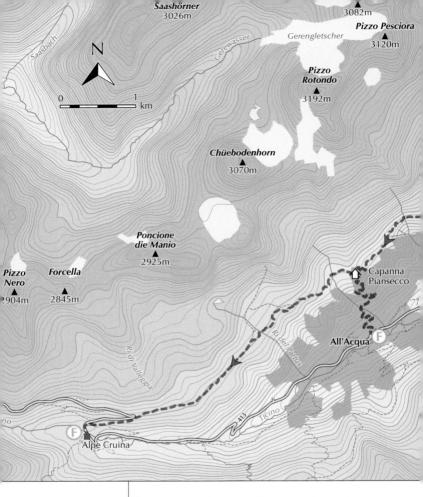

farm buildings that you will see up to the R, above the track. After another 30 min you pass a major track junction marking the route up the Passo di Lucendro; 5 min further on, the next junction marks the way down to the village of Villa Bedretto (see below). From this junction, carry on along the vehicle track for another hour or so

until you reach the junction for the path down to Ronco (L) – reached shortly after the vehicle track has petered out into a footpath. ▶ After 50 min the path brings you out right by the bus stop in **Ronco** and the welcoming and cosy Hotel Stella Alpina (which has a bar/restaurant).

The path down through the forest is precipitously steep and will be very challenging after rain.

To shorten the walk

The path down to Ronco as described here is one of a number of paths that link the high-level Sentiero Val Bedretto with villages at the bottom of the valley. The first of these paths runs down to the village of Villa Bedretto. For 15 min this route is along a track, until the farm buildings at **Traversa di Cavanna**; here it turns into a forest path that cuts steeply down the valley side, bringing you to **Villa Bedretto** after 35 min. The bus stops on the minor road that threads its way through the village – there's no need to go further down to the main valley road – and although there's a bar in Villa Bedretto it seems to keep rather limited opening hours and is unlikely to be open during the day; there's no shop.

To lengthen the walk

At the Ronco path junction, instead of turning L and heading down the valley to Ronco (as described), keep straight on along the Sentiero Alta. In 1hr 15 min the **Capanna Piansecco** is reached (see Walk 34). There's a path (40 min) down to the village of **All'Acqua** from here; buses operate year-round from All'Acqua to Airolo. However, the Sentiero Alta continues on for another 1 hr 30 min beyond the *capanna* to **Alpe di Cruina**, a lonely bus stop on the road up to the Nufenenpass (Passo della Novena) (no shelter/refreshments; a total of 5 hr 45 min from the Gotthard Pass summit). Note that buses only serve this stop between late June and mid October; the service is infrequent so check times before embarking on this route. Much of the section between Capanna Piansecco and Alpe di Cruina is rocky underfoot, with a few streams to ford and with regular climbs and descents – though the far-from-anywhere remoteness, and the views over the valley, more than make up for this.

WALK 31

*Circuit of lakes at the summit
of the St Gotthard Pass*

Start/finish	Gotthard Passhöhe bus stop
Distance	12.5km (7.75 miles)
Ascent/descent	470m
Difficulty	Grade 3
Walking time	4 hr
Terrain	Metalled roads and vehicle tracks in first section but mainly rocky mountain paths thereafter, challenging in a couple of places
Refreshments	Only available at start/finish.

The summit of the St Gotthard Pass may be a tourist merry-go-round – see Walk 30 for a run-down of the history of the pass and the current facilities and attractions there – but it's easy to get away from the bustle and into the wild countryside that surrounds the Pass. This walk, which takes in a circuit of the lakes to the northwest of the summit, is by far the most popular way to do this. There's a steep ascent up to the lakes from the artificial Lago di Lucendro, but once that's done the paths that fringe jewel-like Laghi Valletta, Laghi Orsirora and Lago d'Orsino, all set in rocky basins amidst high countryside, are for the main part relatively level and easy-going, allowing walkers to enjoy some raw and expansive scenery. You'll need to keep an eye on the weather at this high altitude – this is one of only a couple of walks in this book that take you higher than 2400m – and beware that even if it's a warm sunny day in Airolo, chill winds funnel through the pass and you would be ill-advised to attempt this walk without warm clothing.

ACCESS

The Gotthard Passhöhe bus stop, served by 5 daily buses from Airolo in summer, is situated beside the main cluster of restaurants and car parks at the top of the St Gotthard Pass.

The first track marker post can be found adjacent to the Guex monument (see Walk 30) beside the bus stop at the summit of the pass. This sign directs you R (NE) towards the Passo di Lucendro, along a vehicle track that hugs the eastern shoreline of the small, circular lake at the summit of the pass. Heading past the stalls selling barbecued bratwurst and cuddly-toy St Bernard dogs you pass a second marker post indicating the route to the Laghi d'Orsirora, the highest of the four natural lakes the walk passes. As the road curls round to the NW and leaves the lake shore, ignore the turning to the L and head past the barrier and along the track as it runs adjacent to the busy road that forms the northerly approach to the pass.

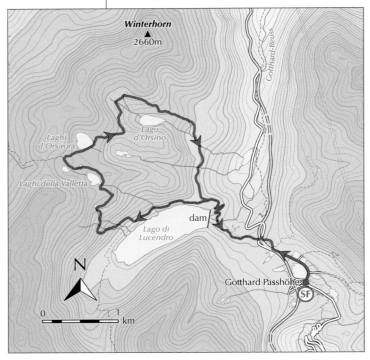

As the track dips down, head L under the main road through a short tunnel and then carry on along this road to the hydroelectric **dam** holding back the **Lago di Lucendro**. You cross the lake's outflow on a bridge at the base of the dam, after which you ascend a track that zig-zags steeply up the valley side towards the crest of the dam. As the path levels off ignore the turning (R) that drops down to the N; instead, carry on W along the main track to reach the northern shore of the Lago di Lucendro. The shoreline path now levels out for a while before you arrive at a track junction (reached some 50 min from the Pass) with a R turn signposted to Lago d'Orsino.

This is the start of a steep ascent up the valley side. Reckon on 45 min to reach the viewpoint over the **Laghi della Valletta**, the first of the four natural lakes that the walk passes (you pass a smaller, un-named lake – which is really not much more than a pond – on the way). From the viewpoint the path drops down to the shores of the lake before heading up along the steep slope that flanks its eastern side. Around 15 min later you pass the second natural lake of the walk, also un-named (keeping to its R) before reaching a track junction (marked by signs on a rock, rather than on a post) that sends you R (E) towards Laghi d'Orsirora. This path now crests a ridge that, at 2482m, is the highest point of the walk.

Immediately beyond the ridge is the **Laghi d'Orsirora** itself. ▶ The path skirts the lake's southern shore and crests another low ridge before a steep – sometimes pre-cipitously so – descent down to the slopes that flank the Lago d'Orsino, the largest of the four lakes. The path circles the broad, natural bowl in which the lake sits, heading N then E: around 50 min after leaving the shores of Laghi d'Orsirora you arrive at the eastern end of **Lago d'Orsino**, with a view that now opens up along the valley towards your starting point and destination, the distant cluster of buildings around the summit of the St Gotthard Pass (still another 1 hr 20 min away).

There's another steep descent to contend with now before the route follows a level path along the southern flank of the valley. ▶ A final short, sharp uphill section

This is the most beautifully-situated of the lakes; on fine days its shores are popular with picnickers.

There's a good view from this path over the extensive galleries that protect the main road up to the Gotthard Pass from avalanches and landslides.

The Laghi d'Orsirora is the most beautiful of the lakes the walk passes

brings you to the track above the **dam**, which you were on before: for the last 40 min you must retrace your steps, heading down the zig-zags to the base of the dam, and then along the track that curls under the main road and skirts the lake at the summit of the pass, bringing you back past the cuddly St Bernard dogs and the barbecued bratwurst stalls to the **Gotthard Passhöhe** bus stop.

WALK 32

Sentiero Bassa Val Bedretto

Start	All'Acqua Bus Stop
Finish	Airolo Railway Station
Distance	13.5km (8.5miles)
Ascent	90m
Descent	560m
Difficulty	Grade 2
Walking time	3 hr 50 min
Terrain	Easy woodland paths throughout
Refreshments	There are restaurants in All'Acqua and Ronco, but no shops anywhere along the route (until you reach Airolo).

This straightforward walk along the Val Bedretto takes walkers through typically attractive valley-bottom scenery – meadowland, woodland and tiny villages – along an easy succession of farm tracks and forest paths (the grading 2 comes from the length of the walk rather than the difficulty of the terrain). The route is mostly well marked, the gradients are minimal and this walk might well be a good bet for the start of your holiday as you ease yourself into Ticino walking. Alternatively, it's a good option when poor weather makes walking at higher levels unattractive – and the low altitude means that the walk is also free of snow for most of the year.

ACCESS

Buses (every 1–3 hours in summer) run from outside Airolo station to All'Acqua.

The bus from Airolo will drop you at an extensive layby in **All'Acqua**, which is little more than a skinny scattering of buildings spread along the roadside. The most prominent building in the village is the Ristorante All'Acqua (meals and accommodation), though don't miss the tiny, starkly

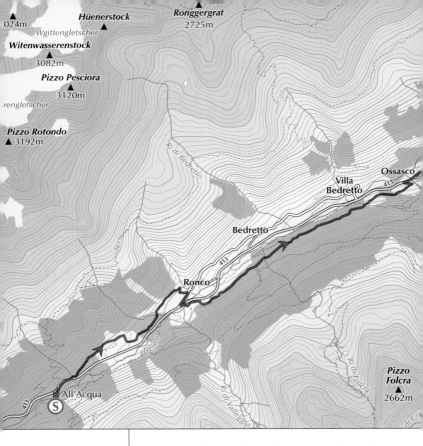

modern roadside chapel just to its southwest. The marker post by the bus stop sends you back along the road for a couple of minutes and then L along a side road; keep looking for the signs reading *sentiero* as the path hugs the N side of the valley before it heads back towards the road and enters some woodland.

Marking in the woodland stretch could be better: where the path divides, take the R fork which leads gently downhill – you'll know you're on the right track if, some moments later, you find yourself crossing a stream

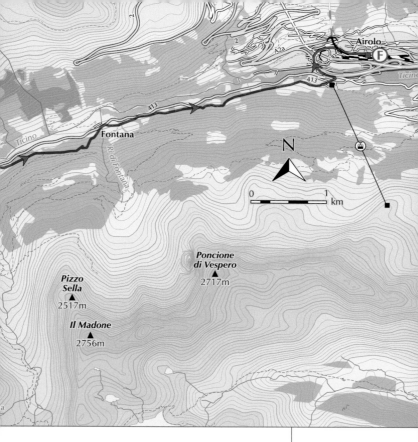

beside a small hut. From here head on up through some farm buildings and along a terrace cut into the valley side, overlooking a lake and a small industrial concern (you'll see diggers and piles of quarried stone). The path then drops down to the minor road that threads through the villages in this part of the valley; here, 40 min from All'Acqua, you are just outside the hamlet of **Ronco**. ▶ To continue the walk, at the minor road turn R, which brings you down to the main road that runs along the valley floor.

On reaching the minor road you can turn L to head into Ronco itself: after barely a minute you arrive at the Stella Alpina Restaurant and bus stop.

Ronco, as seen from the walk

Less lovely are the sturdy defences (banks and concrete walls built over the valley's lower flanks) that protect these villages from avalanches.

Turn L at the main road, cross the bridge and then follow the marker post that sends you R up a short rise to join a farm track. The next 1 hr 15 min (to Ossasco) is the most attractive part of the walk, with views across the river to succession of villages that cluster the N flank – Ronco, followed by **Bedretto** and then **Villa Bedretto** – whose pastel-coloured houses look lovely in the sun. ◄ Track marking is good in this section, though watch carefully at junctions – a myriad of tracks criss-cross each other along this part of the valley.

The route drops down to the village of **Ossasco** and passes some traditional burnt-wood houses before heading up across some meadowland (look for yellow and black poles that mark the way here) and into a pine forest. Some 30 min later the path drops down to the road again, at **Fontana**; the road here is narrow but cars navigate through the village slowly and there is marked space on the road for pedestrians.

Beyond the village the route once again heads up (R) onto the lower flanks of the valley. The curling road up to the Gotthard Pass is now visible on the opposite side of the valley, which soon becomes busy with infrastructure – electricity pylons and roads coiling up the slopes – as you approach the restaurant at the base station of the Airolo-Pesciüm cable car (1 hr from Fontana).

Head past the cable car station and down some steps beside a multi-storey carpark to the road – there's a confusing (and hideously ugly) jumble of sliproads and junctions here, but the road that curls round and into **Airolo** has a pavement all the way. You reach the railway station 20 min after leaving the cable car base station. ▸

Look R as you walk along this road to see where it runs right above the entrance portals to the two (motorway and rail) Gotthard tunnels.

WALK 33
Along the Val Torta to Capanna Cristallina

Start	Pesciüm cable car station
Finish	Ossasco bus Stop
Distance	18.5km (11.5miles)
Ascent	1080m
Descent	1510m
Difficulty	Grade 3
Walking time	7 hr 30 min
Terrain	Vehicle tracks and woodland paths rising to rocky mountain trails, challenging in places and with snow patches to cross
Refreshments	Eating options are limited to the restaurant beside the cable car station at Pesciüm, and the Capanna Cristallina; buy snacks and drinks before setting out from Airolo.

This challenging but thoroughly rewarding day-long walk takes you up through the tranquil Val Torta to the Capanna Cristallina, a spectacularly situated and recently built mountain hut situated at the summit of the pedestrian-only Passo di Cristallina. The cable car from Airolo relieves you of some of the climbing, but nonetheless it's a tough ascent, recommended for the fit and experienced – and it is likely that there will be sloping snowfields to cross as you approach the hut, so walking poles and adequate shoes are a necessity. Note that the Capanna Cristallina can also be approached from Robiei at the head of one of the Locarno valleys (see Walk 16) – and in fact many do the walk in two stages, walking to the hut from Robiei, staying overnight, and then walking down to Ossasco the next day.

ACCESS

Pesciüm is reached by cable car from Airolo (the lower station is a 20-min walk from the railway station, or take a bus to Funivia); Ossasco is linked by bus to Airolo every 1–3 hours (20 min).

From the cable car station at **Pesciüm** pick up the signs for Alpe di Cristallina, walking past the large restaurant complex and then taking the farm track that leads L, gently uphill. The track winds slowly down through larch forests for an hour or so until a junction sends you off L up a steep path that rises through the trees (look for the red-and-white markings on rocks, and the sign reading *sentiero*). This path reaches a farm track once more at **Piano di Pescia**. From the farm buildings here it's 20 min to **Alpe di Cristallina** (1 hr 50 min from Pesciüm), a major track junction beside some extensive farm buildings.

The climb begins here (the track marker post for 'Capanna Cristallina' is behind the farm buildings). You should reckon on 3 hours of fairly relentless ascent up to the *capanna* as the path climbs up past the treeline and alongside the Cristallina river, whose burbling mingles with the familiar sounds of cowbells from the wandering herds who are kept on these summer pastures. You'll see the *capanna*, spectacularly perched in the saddle of

Map continues on page 226

Airolo

Ticino

413

Ticino

413

Rio di Fontana

Pesciüm

S

Sasso della Boggia

Piano di Pescia

Poncione di Vespero
▲
2717m

Pizzo Sella
▲
2517m

N

0   1
└────────┘ km

The final approach to the Capanna Cristallina

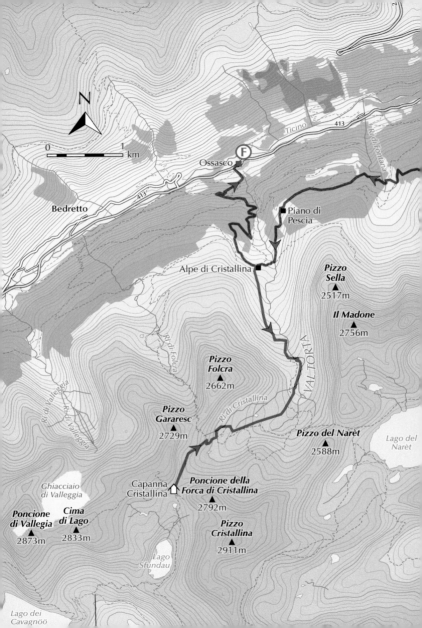

the pass, as the path swings around to the southwest, but don't be deceived – it's still a good hour away.

On the final ascent, be wary of the track junction from which a route leads northwest, over a low pass into the Val Cassinello: this is not a designated walking path and so it is not marked by an official track marker post, and it is also not the route to the *capanna*. (The correct route to the *capanna* is marked by a sign painted on the rock.) So long as you keep the **capanna** (see Walk 16) in your sights you shouldn't go wrong. Unless you are here at the end of a long warm summer the last few hundred metres will involve crossing snowfields.

To return, retrace your steps from the *capanna* to Alpe di Cristallina (2 hr) and then turn L (NW) along the farm track signposted to Ronco. Within 10 min a sign will point you R to Ossasco – first along a track, and then after 30 min another sign will direct you along steeply sloping woodland paths which brings you after another 30 min to a small parking area beside the bus stop at the roadside village of **Ossasco**. ▶

Unfortunately there's no pub or shop here, but the water fountains in the village and at the parking area itself will at least allow you to refill your water bottles.

WALK 34
Nufenenpass and the Upper Val Bedretto

Start	Nufenen Passhöhe bus stop
Finish	All'Acqua bus stop
Distance	10.75km (6.75 miles)
Ascent	120m
Descent	990m
Difficulty	Grade 2
Walking time	3 hr 35 min
Terrain	High meadowland and forest paths, often rocky underfoot
Refreshments	There is a café at the Nufenenpass summit, and at the destination bus stop you'll find the Ristorante All'Acqua (closed Tues and Weds); en route, refreshments are available at the Capanna Piansecco.

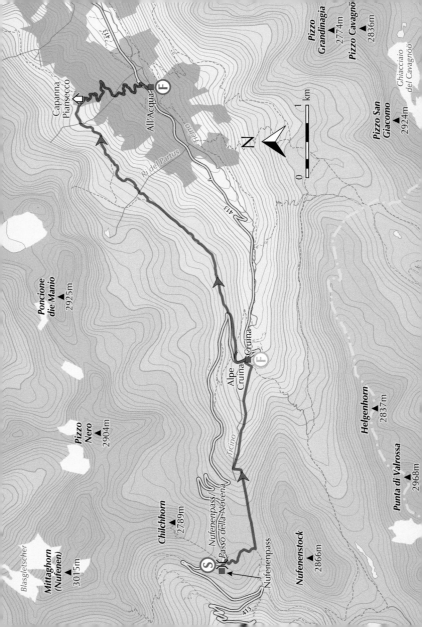

The Passo della Novena – better known by its German name, the Nufenenpass – links Canton Ticino with Canton Valais. The latter is a predominantly French-speaking Canton but its northeastern end is German-speaking, hence the 'Wilkommen' sign at the top of the pass – which, situated at an altitude of 2478m, is the highest pass with a paved road within Switzerland. From the parking area by the café there is a panoramic view of the Bernese Alps. This walk starts at the bus stop and café here and quickly joins the Ticino river when it is nothing but a mountain stream, giving a taste of a high Alpine environment (with occasional snow patches) before dropping down to lower altitudes as the valley widens and the bare, goat-grazed mountainsides gradually become meadowland and then woodland. The scenery throughout is dramatic – verging on the overwhelming – but there is little by way of ascent (since the walk starts at such a high altitude) and there are opportunities to shorten the walk if need be (at Cruina, where the route crosses the road up to the pass at a bus stop). The Capanna Piansecco also allows for a break at a valleyside mountain hut shortly before the walk's end. Note that an area of trails to the southwest of the Pass has been closed because of landslides, making access to the Griesee and its dam, and the Val Corno to the east, much more difficult than it might otherwise be.

ACCESS

Bus #B111 operates four times daily from Airolo to the Nufenenpass (journey time 45 min) and every 1–3 hours from All'Acqua to Airolo (journey time 24 min).

The track marker post at the pass summit, situated a little way along the road back down to Airolo, points the way S over a knuckle of rock, taking walkers into a silent world well away from the bustle of the pass. After 10 min a track marker post at a prominent junction points L (E). There are small patches of snow to cross here, but as the path drops down and joins the Ticino river (to the L) the high Alpine environment is left behind and the valley opens out, with the farm buildings at Alpe Cruina visible in the distance around 20 min from the marker post. ▶ A minute or so from the farm buildings and the road at **Alpe**

This is a beautiful and dramatic valley, with the bubbling Ticino river giving a sense of the geographical context of this remote part of the canton.

Walkers' first view of Cruina, and the road up to the Pass

Cruina you are signed L to the Capanna Piansecco at a track marker post (1 hr 10 min from the Pass summit).

The path crosses the main road here, at **Cruina bus stop** – a place to cut short the walk if need be, though there is nowhere to shelter and buses (travelling between the Pass and Airolo) are infrequent. Note that a path also runs from here along the valley floor to All'Acqua, taking 1 hr 15 min – much less time than the route outlined below, with none of the ascent, though taking this route means that you bypass the *capanna*.

At Cruina you must walk along the road for a short way as it crosses the Ticino river. Then you are sent (R) on a path that rises up to the road's immediate R; where the road turns a hairpin the path abandons it for the quiet of the valley sides. Once the ascent is done the path undulates along the valley side at around the 2100m contour, with the *capanna* visible straight ahead of you on the hillside around an hour from Alpe Cruina.

This part of the route takes you across open pasture, with great views across the valley as the massif to the N towers over you. However, the main valley-bottom road (and river) are obscured by the topography of the valley side, lending a real sense of isolation to this second part of the walk.

Ignore the tracks that on occasions lead L up to lakes tucked into folds of the valley sides: instead continue straight on, reaching the **Capanna Piansecco** around 1 hr 45 min from Cruina. ▶ From the *capanna* a well-made path zig-zags down the hill through the woods, after 40 min you reach the main road at **All'Acqua** beside the pastel-green Ristorante. Buses stop in the layby 100m up the road.

The capanna (**www.capannapiansecco.ch**), situated at the tree line with a backdrop of peaks rising to 3000m, was completely renovated in 2020 and attractively refaced in pine, concrete and pale stone.

WALK 35
Strada Alta Valle Leventina (north side)

Start	Airolo railway station
Finish	Faido railway station
Distance	18km (11 miles)
Ascent	520m
Descent	900m
Difficulty	Grade 2
Walking time	5 hr 30 min
Terrain	Woodland paths, metalled roads and vehicle tracks predominate
Refreshments	There are no shops in any of the villages. Stock up on drinks and snacks in Airolo. The only eating place you'll find is at Altanca, around a third of the way into the walk.

The Strada Alta Valle Leventina is the 'high road' of the North side of the Leventina valley, linking the various villages and hamlets that perch amidst forest and pastureland on the valley's upper terraces. (The complete Strada Alta runs all the way from Airolo to Biasca and is some 45km in length; the part presented here is the first and most scenic section of the walk.) The walk is well signed throughout and runs partly along quiet roads and partly along gently graded forest tracks; however, the downhill section between Lurengo and Freggio is steep and rocky in places, hence this walk has been given a difficulty designation of 2. The walk is distinguished by the ever-changing views over the Valle Leventina and back towards the approach to the Gotthard, and across the valley to the forbidding Campo Tencia massif. The walk is not particularly high or exposed, making it a good option when cloudy or rainy weather makes other walks in the area less appealing.

ACCESS

Hourly trains and buses link Faido railway station with Airolo.

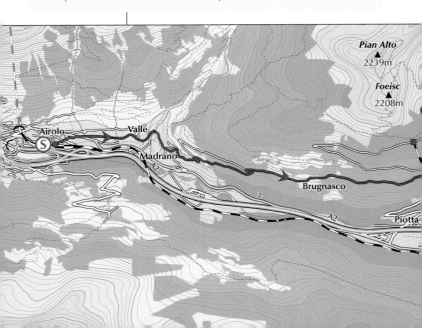

The first route marker is outside the **Airolo** station kiosk. It directs walkers up the road to Airolo's main street (passing the town cinema) and then R through the town's humdrum suburbs. After some 15 min you pass through **Valle**, a settlement that adjoins Airolo – and this is where you pick up the familiar red-and-white wayside track markings. The markings lead you out of Valle, down to cross the River Canaria, and up to the attractive village of **Madrano**, with its burnt-wood chalet-style buildings. Marker posts direct you through the main square and up a flight of steps (from a triangular expanse of cobbles) to a road that heads once again into countryside. After rounding a hairpin bend take the R at the marker post onto a path that climbs relatively steeply up through trees. This is the route's major uphill section: it leads you once again onto the road, and around 50 min from Madrano you pass through the hamlet of **Brugnasco**.

Continuing along the road beyond Brugnasco you pass under the Piotta–Piora funicular railway (see Walk 37; there's a midway station here) before reaching

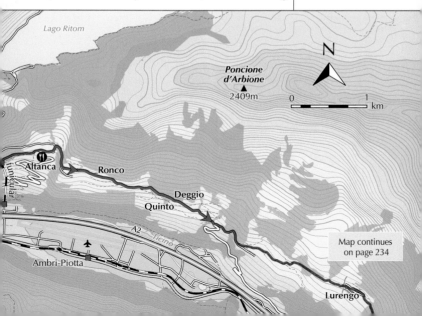

Map continues
on page 234

Altanca is linked by bus to Piotta on the valley floor. Leaving the village you pass the Osteria Altanca, a café/restaurant open daily 8am–11pm, with an attractive outdoor terrace.

Altanca (35 min from Brugnasco), another attractive village. ◄

Beyond Altanca the road – which sees very little traffic – now runs down through the hamlet of **Ronco** (not to be confused with the village of the same name in the Val Bedretto), and some 50 min beyond Altanca brings you to **Deggio**, which like Altanca is linked by bus to Piotta on the valley floor. Just under 10 min beyond Deggio you finally leave the road (look for the junction by a roadside shrine), taking a paved lane up through pastureland. The lane soon becomes a track that leads you to the hamlet of **Lurengo**, reached in around 30 min.

From Lurengo – which also has a bus stop – head along the lane that takes you past an agricultural building fashioned unusually from pastel-pink bricks, and then into the woods. After 20 min a junction sends you R, along the most difficult section of the route: it's steep and rocky underfoot for much of the next hour, down to

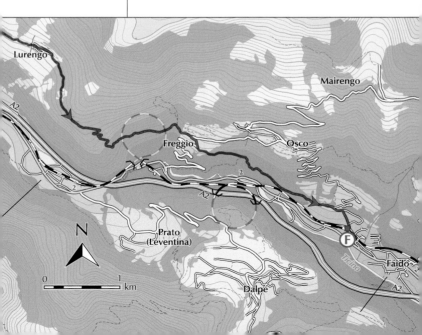

the church at **Freggio**, during which you descend some 350m in altitude.

Freggio is on a road that winds steeply up from the valley floor; follow it from the church down to the first hairpin bend and take the path signed L. This leads you past a large modern farm complex and then along farm tracks and easy forest paths that run down to the bottom of the valley; you reach the first houses in **Faido** some 40 min after leaving Freggio. Next to them is a track marker post that points the way along a minor road and down through more houses to the station (10 min). ▶

The village of Altanca, through which the walk passes

There's nowhere supplying food or drink around the station (bar the station vending machine); the centre of Faido is unfortunately a 600m walk away.

235

WALK 36

Sentiero Alta Valle Leventina (south side)

Start	Pesciüm cable car station
Finish	Tremorgio cable car top station
Distance	14km (8.75 miles)
Ascent	720m
Descent	610m
Difficulty	Grade 2
Walking time	5 hr
Terrain	A mixture of vehicle tracks and woodland paths – however, the last section is marked by a challenging uphill ascent through dense woodland
Refreshments	Only available at the restaurants attached to the two cable car stations.

This walk is along the myriad of tracks that run through the thick forests that cling to the south side of the Valle Leventina, way above the valley floor. Access to the upper slopes is by cable car at either end of the walk – but don't be fooled, there's still a fair amount of climbing to do, particularly at the end of the walk where the route ascends steeply over one of the precipitous spurs of land that cradle beautiful, jewel-like Lago Tremorgio. This lake makes for a fine destination for this walk and is undoubtedly the scenic highlight. Until the final ascent and descent you'll be walking along relatively easy forest paths and vehicle tracks that run along the flanks of the valley, giving superlative views over it. Whereas the Strada Alta that runs along the Valle Leventina's north side passes through a number of villages (see Walk 35), the south side is sparsely settled, and only once on this walk do you pass through anything approaching a hamlet.

ACCESS

Pesciüm cable car station is the midway station of the cable car that rises from Airolo (the base station is a walk of 20 min from Airolo railway station); the lower station of the Tremorgio cable car is a few steps from Rodi Posta bus stop on the Airolo-Biasca-Bellinzona bus route (hourly services).

Pick up the trail right outside the **Pesciüm** cable car station, where a track marker post points out the Sentiero Alto to Tremorgio. The route drops down across a patch of meadowland to the base station of a ski tow, before rising gently into woodland where you should pick up the signs directing you towards the Chalet Polenta Ravina. After around 10 min the path divides: take the R fork to skirt a small lake (the Grasso di Lago, to your R) and carry on along the path as it curves S, with chains and handrails to aid with some of the slippery parts. Some 35 min from Pesciüm you arrive at the base station of a ski tow.

Crossing under the ski tow's cables, keeping a small chalet to your L, cross a vehicle track to reach a marker post that points the way to Lago di Rovina. The route now crosses an area of bogland (look for the short poles that mark the way) before heading once again into the trees. After 10 min a path heads R to Lago di Rovina, Fusio and the Passo Sassello, which you should ignore; instead carry on along the main path, which now gives superlative views across the valley to the Piotta-Piora funicular (see Walk 37).

Some 40 min after the Passo Sassello track junction there's a fairly substantial stream to ford. Moments later there's another track junction, where you should stay on the level, crossing a second river, this time via a bridge. Turning L at the junction that immediately follows, you should pick up the signs for Lago Tremorgio, heading now along a vehicle track: follow it across a second bridge, and ignore the track that rises to the R at the next junction. Keep on the track as it drops down to the farm buildings at **Pian Taiöi** (15 min from the bridges). From here the vehicle track runs E along the valley sides, dropping down steadily; after 40 min you reach the scattered hamlet of **Cassin d'Ambri**, with its typical burnt-wood chalets.

From Cassin d'Ambri the signs to Lago Tremorgio point you along a vehicle track that rises, first gradually, and then via a series of steep hairpins, to the isolated stone house at **Pian Mott** (45 min). From here you're back on forest footpaths. After 15 min take the R fork (up) where the

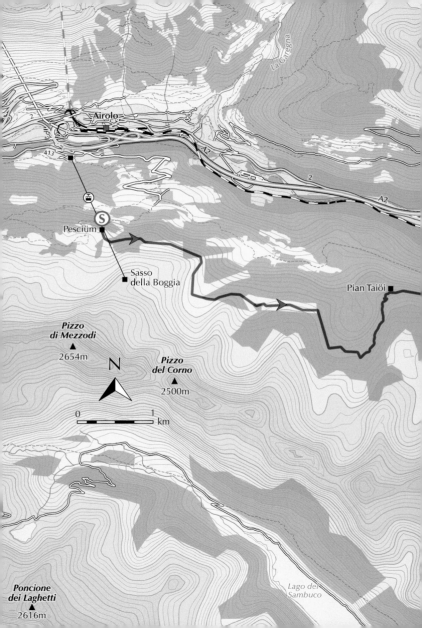

Airolo

413

Pesciüm

S

Sasso
della Boggia

Pian Taiöi

la Garegna

A2

2

A2

2

**Pizzo
di Mezzodi**
▲
2654m

N

**Pizzo
del Corno**
▲
2500m

0   1
└─────────────┘ km

**Poncione
dei Laghetti**
▲
2616m

Lago del
Sambuco

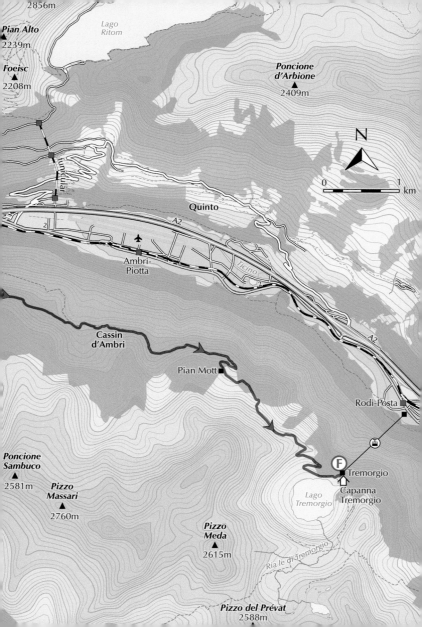

Lago Tremorgio, as seen from the walk

paths divide and ascend the steep promontory of land that juts out from the valley sides. After some 15 min of strenuous climbing the route runs level along the contours for another 15 min, the precipitous drop to the L meaning that this is not the route for vertigo sufferers! Finally the route rises over a last, low spur of land and a view over Lago Tremorgio opens up gloriously below you.

To end the walk, go down to the lake on the zig-zag paths and head L around the southern shore; then take the path that runs behind the farm buildings and across a bridge. A final short climb awaits you, along the path that rises to the R of a building with a grass roof. This path rises to the top station of the **Tremorgio** cable car – which you arrive at some 40 min after the first view of the lake.

The level path that runs SW from the upper cable car station brings you after just 1 min to the **Capanna Tremorgio**, a mountain hut overlooking the lake that will offer accommodation and refreshments. Details are included under Walk 38, for which this is the starting point.

WALK 37
Circuit of Lago Ritom

Start/finish	Piora (upper station of Ritom funicular railway)
Distance	12km (7.5 miles)
Ascent/descent	310m
Difficulty	Grade 2
Walking time	3 hr
Terrain	Mostly vehicle tracks and metalled roads, with some woodland and meadowland paths
Refreshments	There are places to eat around the lower and upper funicular stations and close to the dam – and at the Capanna Cadagno, half-way through the walk.

This classic high-level Ticino walk is easily accessible thanks to the Ritom funicular railway which gives access to Lago Ritom, a beautifully situated lake located at an altitude of 1850m at the foot of some forbidding peaks. The walk takes the form of a circuit of the lake, with the Capanna Cadagno mountain hut allowing for a break at the half-way stage. Gradients are very gentle for the most part, making the walk popular with families. However, with such easy access to such breathtaking scenery (cars can be driven up here, too) the routes are understandably popular and on fine days you certainly won't be the only person enjoying them.

ACCESS

The base station of the Ritom funicular railway is at Piotta, 5km east of Airolo; infrequent buses run there direct from Airolo railway station (route #117 to Dalpe) – otherwise, it's a walk of around 10 min from Piotta Posta bus stop on the Airolo-Biasca-Bellinzona bus route (hourly services).

LAGO RITOM

Lago Ritom was created in its current form in 1918 when the level of the natural lake that was situated in this bowl in the mountains was raised through the construction of a dam, as part of a hydro-electric power scheme to provide electricity for the Gotthard rail line. The funicular, whose top station is 1km from the dam, was built at the same time to facilitate the construction of the enormous pipelines that still run parallel to it. Once the hydro scheme was completed the funicular opened to the public, advertising itself as the steepest funicular railway in the world; it has since been knocked into third place by funiculars at Bern and at Soos near Lake Lucerne, but it remains a mightily impressive piece of engineering, rising 785m with a maximum gradient of 87 per cent. From beside the top station at Piora there are some staggering views over the Valle Leventina, with its array of roads and railways and settlements jostling for space on the flat valley floor alongside the landing strip of Ambri's small, ex-military airport.

Lago Ritom was dammed to provide hydroelectric power

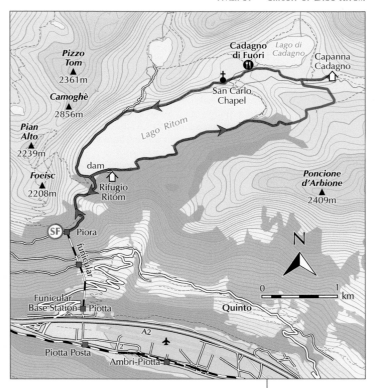

Emerging from the funicular top station at **Piora**, turn R and head along the metalled road. It's narrow and runs through brief tunnels, with cars and pedestrians vying for space along some sections. In 15 min you'll reach the western end of the hydro-electric **dam**. ▶ Cross the dam's crest and from the eastern end set off along the footpath that runs through the forest that girts the lake's southern shore. This is a peaceful path and unlike the road on the lake's north shore, it attracts few walkers.

After 40 min a sign to the Capanna Cadagno points R along a path that rises up through the trees to

At the base of the dam's eastern end is the Rifugo Ritom, a bar-restaurant with accommodation, reachable in 5 min from the western end via a path along the dam's base.

meadowland and a track junction beside a stone hut. Turn L here and follow the path up through a cleft in the ridge of hills. Once you're out of the cleft and into open countryside you'll see the *capanna* down to the L – though reaching it takes longer than you might think, as you need to carry on to the next junction and take the path that leads down through dense foliage to an elegant stone bridge that crosses the Murinascia Grande river. The **capanna** is then accessed up along a track to the right (a total of 1 hr 30 min walking from the dam).

> The **Capanna Cadagno** mountain hut (www.capanna cadagno.ch; 091 868 13 23) will provide snacks and has recently been extended and modernized, with an attractive terrace and basic but very clean dormitories. The buildings below it to the west include a shop where local produce (cheese, cold meats and so on) can be purchased.

From the *capanna* retrace your steps, heading W along a vehicle track past the local produce shop. The track skirts the southern shore of tiny **Lago di Cadagno** and then takes you past some holiday homes at **Cadagno di Fuori**, amongst which is the Ristoro Taneda restaurant. Just beyond the holiday homes you reach a dramatic viewpoint over Lago Ritom. The track runs below the tiny, isolated **San Carlo chapel** and eventually drops down to the lake shore, hugging its northern side; you arrive back at the western end of the dam after an hour's walk from the *capanna*. From the dam simply retrace your steps along the road to the funicular top station at Piora (15 min).

WALK 38

Lago Tremorgio and Capanna Leit

Start/finish	Top station of Tremorgio cable car
Distance	6km (3.75 miles)
Ascent/descent	420m
Difficulty	Grade 2
Walking time	2 hr 30 min
Terrain	Woodland paths rising to challenging rocky mountain trails
Refreshments	At the Capanna Tremorgio and the Capanna Leit.

The cable car at Rodi that whisks walkers up the near-vertical side of the Ticino valley to an altitude of 1800m gives access to jewel-like Lago Tremorgio, set in a natural bowl in the mountainside and surrounded by forests. The walk from here to the Capanna Leit mountain hut, set in wild countryside high above the lake, is justifiably popular – and not too long, being easily accomplishable in a morning or afternoon. In the walk's second stage there's a choice of two routes up to the Capanna Leit, and going up one way and coming down the other seems an obvious choice. Whichever route you pick, the scenery is fabulous. Although the walk is comparatively short, it is steep and rocky in places – hence its designation as difficulty 2 – though signage and route marking is very clear throughout.

ACCESS

The base station of the Lago Tremorgio cable car is a few steps away from Rodi-Posta bus stop (hourly services to Airolo). Be warned that the cable car up to Tremorgio only seats eight people at a time in its cabin; on fine days in summer, and particularly at weekends, be prepared for a wait to get on at the bottom station.

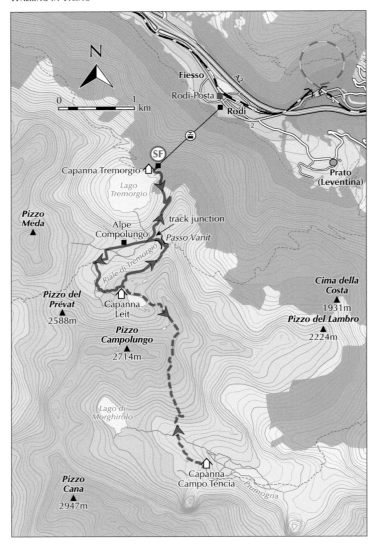

Lago Tremorgio at bottom left, with the capanna hidden by trees to its right

From the top station of the cable car it's barely a minute's level walk to the **Capanna Tremorgio**, set amidst trees on a natural ledge above the lake. ▶ A track marker post outside the *capanna* points the way to Capanna Leit, sending you on a path that climbs steadily up through the forest, providing great views over the lake. After 35 min the path levels out onto open ground and a couple of minutes later you arrive at a major track junction that points out the two different routes up to Capanna Leit.

The slightly longer way (45 min) takes you along the bottom of the Riale di Tremorgio valley, W past the farm buildings at Alpe Campolungo and then L at a junction for the final steep and rocky-under-foot approach to

The Capanna Tremorgio (**www. capannatremorgio. ch**; Tel 091 867 12 52) serves snacks, drinks and basic meals and has an attractive terrace. Accommodation in dormitories is also available.

Capanna Leit, the destination of the walk

In the Riale di Tremorgio valley

the **Capanna Leit** on a path that leads you S and then E around a prominent bluff. ▶

To vary the scenery on the return walk, make your way down from the Capanna Leit via a different path that leads NE and along the Passo Vanit. A L turn at the pass takes you back to the track junction at the top of the climb from Capanna Tremorgio, from where you simply retrace your steps to the start of the walk. This route involves some scrambling over boulders, so if you have children in tow it's probably better to come down from Capanna Leit the way you went up. Whichever way you descend from Capanna Leit, count on just over an hour in total to reach **Capanna Tremorgio** and the cable car station just beyond it.

The Capanna Leit (**www.capanna-leit.ch**; Tel 091 868 1920) offers accommodation, basic snacks and drinks and – of course – there are fine views over the scenery you've just walked through from its terrace.

Extending the walk

This walk could be extended by walking from Capanna Leit to Capanna Campo Tencia, another mountain hut 2 hr 15 min away across challenging terrain; from here a path runs down to the village of Dalpe (2 hr 15 min), which has a limited bus service back to Rodi Posta bus stop – with one late afternoon service even going direct to Airolo.

APPENDIX A
Route summary table

Walk number	Walk name	Start	Grade	Distance	Time	Total ascent	Total descent	Maximum altitude (m)	Page
Walks from Lugano									
1	Lake Lugano shoreline from Paradiso to Gandria	Paradiso debarcadero	1	6.25km	1 hr 45 min	40m	40m	306m	48
2	Campione d'Italia to Cantine di Gandria	Campione d'Italia debarcadero	1	6.75km	2 hr 15 min	200m	200m	472m	53
3	San Salvatore to Morcote	Top station of San Salvatore funicular	2	10km	3 hr 45 min	250m	850m	882m	59
4	Monte Caslano	Caslano debarcadero	2	6.5km	2 hr	250m	250m	518m	64
5	Monte San Giorgio	Top station of Brusino-Arsizio to Serpiano cable car	2	7.25km	2 hr 30 min	500m	500m	1097m	68
6	Monte Tamaro to Monte Lema	Top station of the Monte Tamaro cable car (Alpe Foppa)	3	12.5km	5 hr 30 min	850m	820m	1961m	73
7	Monte Boglia and the Denti della Vecchia	Brè Paese bus stop	3	14km	5 hr 30 min	1150m	860m	1516m	78
8	Monte Bar and the Capriasca Valley	Cortiasca Paese bus stop	3	13.25km	5 hr	900m	1200m	1816m	85
9	Cima di Medeglia and the Old Military Road	Isone Gròssa bus stop	2	11.5km	4 hr	570m	850m	1260m	90

Walk number	Walk name	Grade	Start	Distance	Time	Total ascent	Total descent	Maximum altitude (m)	Page
Walks from Locarno									
10	Along the shore of Lake Maggiore	1	Delta Maggia bus stop	6km	1 hr 20 min	-	-	202m	103
11	Sentiero Collina Alta and Sentiero Collina Bassa	2	Top station of the Madonna del Sasso funicular	13.5km	4 hr	440m	440m	642m	107
12	Cimetta to Mergoscia via Capanna dei Monti di Lego	2	Top station of Cimetta chairlift	11.75km	4 hr 15 min	350m	1260m	1869m	113
13	The Centovalli from Camedo to Intragna	2	Camedo railway station	10.5km	4hr	500m	700m	824m	117
14	The Valle del Salto	2	Maggia Centro bus stop	8km	3 hr 30 min	640m	640m	877m	122
15	Along the Val Lavizzara from Fusio to Bignasco	2	Fusio Paese bus stop	17.75km	5 hr 15 min	360m	1210m	1290m	125
16	Capanna Cristallina from Robiei	3	Upper station of San Carlo-Robiei cable car	12km	4 hr	770m	770m	2575m	132
17	Bosco Gurin to Cimalmotto	2	Top station of Bosco Gurin to Rossboda chairlift	6.5km	3 hr	240m	840m	2222m	136
18	Sentiero per l'Arte	1	Ganne bus stop	4.5km	1 hr 20 min	-	130m	673m	141
19	Revöira and Ca d Dént	2	Lavertezzo Paese bus stop	4km	1 hr 30 min	420m	340m	960m	144
20	Lavertezzo to the Verzasca Dam	2	Lavertezzo Paese bus stop	11.5km	4 hr	550m	600m	890m	148

Walk number	Walk name	Start	Grade	Distance	Time	Total ascent	Total descent	Maximum altitude (m)	Page
Walks from Bellinzona and Biasca									
21	Monte Carasso, Sementina and the Ponte Tibetano	Monte Carasso Cunvént bus stop	2	8.25km	3 hr 30 min	760m	760m	782m	158
22	Capanna Genzianella and Motto della Croce	Artore bus stop	2	12.75km	5 hr 45 min	1190m	1190m	1494m	162
23	The 'Iron Route' from Carena	Carena bus stop	2	14km	5 hr	770m	770m	1677m	167
24	Mornera and the Capanna Albagno	Mornera cable car top station	2	6km	2 hr 30 min	530m	530m	1869m	171
25	Camorino and the Hunger Towers	Camorino Villagio bus stop	1	5.25km	1 hr 40 min	280m	280m	539m	174
26	Capanna Brogoldone and the Santa Maria Monastery	Top station of the Monti-Savorù cable car	2	10.75km	5 hr	650m	1660m	1903m	177
27	Val Blenio Sentiero Storico	Olivone Posta bus stop	2	19km	4 hr 30 min	190m	700m	905m	182
28	Val Blenio Strada Alta	Top station of the Leontica-Cancorì-Pian Nara chairlift	2	13.75km	4 hr	280m	1330m	1967m	190
29	Lukmanier Pass to Olivone via Passo di Gana Negra	Lukmanier Passhöhe bus stop	3	17km	5 hr 30 min	520m	1540m	2430m	195

Walk number	Walk name	Start	Grade	Distance	Time	Total ascent	Total descent	Maximum altitude (m)	Page
Walks from Airolo									
30	Sentiero Alta Val Bedretto	Gotthard Passhöhe bus stop	2	14km	3 hr 45 min	180m	780m	2115m	208
31	Circuit of lakes at the summit of the St Gotthard Pass	Gotthard Passhöhe bus stop	3	12.5km	4 hr	470m	470m	2482m	215
32	Sentiero Bassa Val Bedretto	All'Acqua bus stop	2	13.5km	3 hr 50 min	90m	560m	1615m	219
33	Along the Val Torta to Capanna Cristallina	Pesciüm cable car station	3	18.5km	7 hr 30 min	1080m	1510m	2575m	223
34	Nufenenpass and the Upper Val Bedretto	Nufenen Passhöhe bus stop	2	10.75km	3 hr 35 min	120m	990m	2497m	227
35	Strada Alta Valle Leventina (north side)	Airolo railway station	2	18km	5 hr 30 min	520m	900m	1421m	231
36	Sentiero Alta Valle Leventina (south side)	Pesciüm cable car station	2	14km	5 hr	720m	610m	2036m	236
37	Circuit of Lago Ritom	Piora	2	12km	3 hr	310m	310m	2050m	241
38	Lago Tremorgio and Capanna Leit	Top station of Tremorgio cable car	2	6km	2 hr 30 min	420m	420m	2257m	245

APPENDIX B
Useful contacts

Emergency services

Police
117

Fire
118

Ambulance
144

Swiss Rescue (helicopter rescue in mountain areas)
1414

Tourist information

Main tourist information website
www.ticino.ch

Airolo
tel 0869 1533
www.airolo.ch
Office: in the railway station
Open Mon–Fri 8.30am–noon and
1–5pm; Sat 8.30am–noon; closed Sun

Bellinzona
tel 091 825 2131
www.bellinzonaevalli.ch
Office: Piazza Collegiata 12
Open Mon–Fri 9am–6pm; Sat
9am–4pm; Sun 10am–4pm

Locarno
tel 0848 091091
www.ascona-locarno.com
Office: in the railway Station
Open Mon–Sat 9am–6pm (from 10am
Sat); Sun 10am–1.30pm and 2.30–5pm
(no lunchtime closure July and August)

Lugano
tel 058 220 6506
www.luganoregion.com
Office: Piazza della Riforma 1
(in the Palazzo Civico)
Open Mon–Sat 9am–noon and 1–6pm
(to 5pm Sat); Sun 10am–noon and
1–4pm

Public transport providers

www.tilo.ch
Regional cross-border train services

www.sbb.ch
National rail network, with itinerary
planning and ticket booking for all
public transport

www.postauto.ch
Postbus network

www.tplsa.ch
Lugano city buses

www.fartiamo.ch
Locarno city buses; buses in the
Locarno Valleys; Centovalli rail line

www.autolinee.ch
Bus services between Biasca and the
Val Olivone

www.luganoairport.ch
Lugano airport

www.lakelugano.ch
Boat services on Lake Lugano

Weather

http://www.meteocentrale.ch/

APPENDIX C
Glossary of Italian words

Italian pronunciation is straightforward, since every word is spoken exactly as it is written and usually enunciated clearly. The only slight difficulties come in the following consonants which are different from English:

c before e or i is an English ch: the town of Cevio is chevio

ch is an English k: the town of Chironico is kee-ron-i-co

g before e or i is an English j – Maggiore is madge-or-eh

g before h is 'hard' as in goat

gli as in billion: the village of Miglieglia is Mil-yel-ya

gn as in canyon: the town of Mogno is Monyo

h is silent

sci as in sheep

sce as in shell

z (end of word) as in the ts of 'rats'

z (beginning of word) as in the ds of 'suds'

Vowel sounds are generally easy to get used to:

a – usually long, as in 'art', but occasionally short as in 'atlas'

e – short as as in 'fell'

i – short as in 'injury'

o – usually short, as in 'pot', but occasionally long, as in 'sort'

u – as the 'oo' in 'look'

Note that when ci, gi and sci are followed by a, o or u, the 'i' is not sounded – a classic case being the name 'Giovanni' (pronounced joh-vahn-nee).

The stress of any word usually falls on the second to last syllable, unless a vowel is accented, in which case that is where the stress falls.

Basic words and phrases

English	Italian
yes	*si*
no	*no*
OK	*va bene*
please	*per favore*
thank you (very much)	*(molte) grazie*
you're welcome	*prego*
good morning	*buongiorno*
good evening	*buona sera*
good night	*buona notte*
hello!	*salve!*
hi!	*ciao!*
goodbye!	*arrivederci!*
bye!	*ciao!*
excuse me	*mi scusi*

English	Italian
I'm sorry	*mi dispiace*
enjoy your meal	*buon appetito*
do you speak English?	*parla inglese?*
does anyone here speak English?	*c'è qualcuno che parla inglese?*
I (don't) speak Italian	*io (non) parlo italiana*
I (don't) understand	*(non) capisco*
please write it down	*può scriverlo, per favore?*
can you show me on the map?	*può mostrarmelo sulla carta, per favore?*

Directions and travel

English	Italian
left	*sinistra*
right	*destra*
straight on	*sempre diritto*
east	*est*
south	*sud*
north	*nord*
west	*ovest*
first	*il primo*
last	*l'ultimo*
ticket office	*sportello*
ticket	*biglietto*
day card	*carta giornaliera*
one-way ticket	*solo andata*

English	Italian
return ticket	*di andante e ritorno*
supplement	*sovratassa*
platform	*binario*
departure	*partenza*
arrival	*arrive*
near/far	*vicino/lontano*
broad/narrow	*largo/stretto*
quick/slow	*rapido/lento*
postbus	*autopostale*
bus stop	*fermata*
town/village centre (on bus stops)	*paese*
train	*treno*
station	*stazione*
information	*informazione*
what is the platform for the train to Milan?	*da quale binario parte il treno per Milano?*
what time does the train arrive in Milan?	*quando arriva il treno arrive a Milano?*
change at Giubiasco	*cambiare a Giubiasco*
toilets	*gabinetti*
women's toilet	*signore*
men's toilet	*signori*
(rental) car	*automobile (a noleggio)*
parking area	*parcheggio*

English	Italian
covered car park	*autosilo*
available/full	*libero/occupato*
police	*polizia*
fire service	*pompieri*
ambulance	*ambulanza*
breakdown	*panna*
boat travel	*navigazione*
(rental) bike	*bicicletta (a noleggio)*
mountain bike	*rampichino*
airport	*aeroporto*

Hotels and shops

English	Italian
entrance/exit	*entrata/uscita*
emergency exit	*uscita di sicurezza*
information	*informazione*
push/pull	*spingere/tirare*
reception	*ricezione*
I reserved a room	*ho riservato una camera*
have you got…?	*avete…?*
I'd like…	*vorrei…*
a single room	*camera singola*
a double room	*camera doppia*
with a balcony	*con balcone*
with a shower	*con doccia*
with a bath	*con bagno*
without	*senza*

English	Italian
how much is the room?	*quanto costa la camera?*
with breakfast	*con prima colazione*
with half board	*mezza pensione*
dormitory	*dormitorio*
campsite	*campeggio*
fully booked	*completo*
hot/cold	*caldo/freddo*
open/closed	*aperto/chiuso*
big/small	*grande/piccolo*
opening hours	*orari d'apertura*
day off	*giorno di riposo*
forbidden	*proibito/vietato*

Numbers

English	Italian
0	*zero*
half	*mezzo*
1	*uno*
2	*due*
3	*tre*
4	*quattro*
5	*cinque*
6	*sei*
7	*sette*
8	*otto*
9	*nove*

English	Italian
10	dieci
11	undici
12	dodici
13	tredici
14	quattordici
15	quindici
16	sedici
17	diciasette
18	diciotto
19	diciannove
20	venti
21	ventuno
22	ventidue
30	trenta
40	quaranta
50	cinquanta
60	sessanta
70	settanta
80	ottanta
90	novanta
100	cento
101	un centouno
200	duecento
1000	mille
2000	duemila

Days and months

English	Italian
Monday	lunedi (lu)
Tuesday	martedi (ma)
Wednesday	mercoledi (me)
Thursday	giovedi (gi)
Friday	venerdi (ve)
Saturday	sabato (sa)
Sunday	domenica (do)
day	giorno
in the morning	la mattina
in the afternoon	di pomeriggio
in the evening	di sera
at night	di notte
yesterday	ieri
today	oggi
tomorrow	domani
week	settimana
month	mese
year	anno
spring	primavera
summer	estate
autumn	autunno
winter	inverno
January	gennaio
February	febbraio
March	marzo
April	aprile

English	Italian
May	*maggio*
June	*giugno*
July	*luglio*
August	*agosto*
September	*settembre*
October	*ottobre*
November	*novembre*
December	*dicembre*

Terms useful on walks

English	Italian
forest	*bosco*
alpine hut (with guardian)	*capanna*
castle	*castello*
town centre	*centro*
historic part of town	*centro storico*
church	*chiesa*
river	*fiume*
rustic country inn	*grotto*
lake	*lago*
rustic country inn	*osteria*
market	*mercato*
museum	*museo*
store	*negozio*
town or city hall	*palazzo civico*
danger!	*pericolo!*

English	Italian
town square	*piazza*
peak	*piz*
bridge	*ponte*
alpine hut (with no guardian present)	*rifugio*
restaurant	*ristorante*
ruins	*rovine*
footpath	*sentiero*
Switzerland	*Svizzera*
street	*via*
pedestrian zone	*zona pedonale*
tower	*torre*
tourist office	*uffizio di turismo*

The Capanna Gorda makes for a good midway stop on Walk 28

DOWNLOAD THE ROUTES
IN GPX FORMAT

All the routes in this guide are available for download from:

www.cicerone.co.uk/1060/GPX

as standard format GPX files. You should be able to load them into most online GPX systems and mobile devices, whether GPS or smartphone. You may need to convert the file into your preferred format using a conversion programme such as gpsvisualizer.com or one of the many other such websites and programmes.

When you follow this link, you will be asked for your email address and where you purchased the guidebook, and have the option to subscribe to the Cicerone e-newsletter.

www.cicerone.co.uk

LISTING OF CICERONE GUIDES

For full information on all our guides, books and eBooks, visit our website:
www.cicerone.co.uk